Art Engaging Gangs

Curated by Holly Crawford

June 6 – July 27, 2013

Design by Nicole Bebout

AC Institute

Since its inception in 2004, the AC Institute's mission has been to advance the understanding of the arts through investigation, research and education. It is a lab and forum for experimentation and critical discussion. We support and develop projects that explore a performative exchange across visual, sonic, verbal and experiential disciplines. We encourage critical writing that challenges conventional expectations of meaning and objectivity as well as the boundaries between the rational and subjective.

The AC Institute is a nonprofit 501(c)(3) organization under the direction of Holly Crawford.

Table of Contents

They Have Gone Awry: Contemporary Portraiture of the Other

Holly Crawford

"These strangely ordinary and disdainfully familiar sights cruelly sting my unconsidered eyes…" Marcel Proust, *Remembrance of Things Past*

Sociologist Sudhir Venkatesh mused in his book *Gang Leader for a Day*, "When I saw a group of people huddled on a corner, I wondered if they were protecting their turf. I had a lot of questions: Why would anyone join a gang? What were the benefits? Didn't they get bored hanging out in stairwells…."[1] The nine artists in this exhibition —Erik Bergrin, Mark Dillon, Jasmine Johnson, Nadín Ospina, Joseph Rodriguez, Paula Roush, Maayke Schurer, Robert Taub and Zefrey Throwell—have asked themselves these questions and

---

[1] Sudhir Venkatesh, *Gang Leader For A Day, A Rogue Sociologist Takes to the Streets*. New York: The Penguin Press, 2008, p. 27. Sudhir Venkatesh is a professor of Sociology at Columbia University. The title of this book, *Gang Leader For A Day*, is based on a very small and significant part of his years of research. His book is a moving account of how he became involved with members of a Chicago gang and the problems he thought about and encountered more than twenty years ago when he was a graduate student at the University of Chicago. His account of survey research, a staple of sociology, was humorous and moving.

many more about violence, death, drugs and gangs from the perspective of gangs, victims and the larger community as well how to construct a historical archive that defines these issues in the digital age. Their responses and artistic approaches to the issues and situations they raise, be they narrative, descriptive or embedded in personal experiences of the individual, are rendered in different media—painting, photography, sculpture and video. What constitutes political or socially conscious art is generally a calling of attention to or a pointing out of social conditions in a way that is enlightening and critical. This work was not created for shock value. It may appear to be done with that agenda. As Walter Benjamin aptly pointed out, "There is no document of civilization that is not at the same time a document of barbarism."[2] All artists, those included in this exhibition and others, take on a risk when they exhibit their art. But to dismiss this work so quickly would miss the very personal narrative that is embedded in the art by each artist. The question of whether these or other political art is ultimately an effective agent for change is still the elephant in the room.[3] All the work in this exhibition was created with the intent of being perceived both as art and as an outlet for cultural commentary and social critique. As Michael Baxandall pointed out in his incisive social history of quattrocento Italian

---

[2] Walter Benjamin, "Theses on the Philosophy of History," in *Illuminations*. Edited by Hannah Aredt. New York: Harcourt, Brace,1968, p. 153.

[3] See Peter Selz, *Art of Engagement*. Berkeley: University of California Press, 2006; Peter Selz, *Beyond the Mainstream*, Cambridge, Cambridge University Press, 1997; Johanna Drucker, *The Century of Artists' Books*. New York City: Granary Books, 1995.

painting, "the artist depends on the beholder to recognize that the art produced is an integral part of the total culture, of the time, the place, and the social circumstances in which it is made. What was true of the fifteenth–century Florence applies perhaps even more to twentieth century…"[4] The answer to an artwork's effectiveness as both art and cultural critique is left to the contemporary viewer and to the future. These works are readable across the ages; violence, death, sorrow and loss are unfortunately universal and timeless.

This exhibition does not include the work of taggers and other gang street art. Such art is fun and colorful, and now has a long history in contemporary art. Instead, the art in this exhibition looks more specifically at the people touched by gangs: who are they and what happens to them? Who is hurt? This art is about the violence that does happen. They are not the celebrities who fill news stories today. The work looks beyond the news headlines.

One major news story in early 2013 covered the proliferation in Chicago of deadly shootings that occurred during funerals.[5] As Monica Daveys writes in *The New York Times*,

---

[4] Ibid., 26-27.

[5] This exhibition was curated about five to six months before this headline. The story ist one of many that we see. What is happening in Chicago at this time is very tragic event. It is not an unexpected event. And it is not isolated to Chicago. All major cities have gangs. See "18 with a bullet, Gang Violence Around the World," a documentary on gangs worldwide. It was broadcast on PBS in 2008. http://www.pbs.org/wnet/wideangle/episodes/18-with-a-bullet/gang-violence-around-the-world/1392/.

"...the overall rise in killings here blurs another truth: the homicides, most of which the authorities described as gang-against-gang shootings, have not been spread evenly across this city. Instead, they have mostly taken place in neighborhoods north and south of Chicago's gleaming downtown towers."[6] It is easy to think, "Oh, it's just Chicago and it's not in my neighborhood." Many solutions have been suggested and tried at different times--a war on drugs or their legalization, bolstering education, building projects, or jailing the culprits. The jails are full. Projects have been built and torn down. Jobs are exported. Gangs still persist.

What is the etymology of the word 'gang'? Long ago the poet Robert Burns used the word in a poem that has been referenced many times in literature and movies. When he used the word it meant 'to go.' Think of the words 'gangway' and 'gangplank.' In the late nineteenth century 'gangs' was used as a collective verb referring to a group of people. It did not originally have the negative connotation it holds now. Distinctions seem to be made between the smaller, younger gang member on the street and the larger organization. It has been argued that gangs have existed for a long time.

> Gangs have existed for hundreds of years, in many societies. Some anthropologists have argued that the gang is among the oldest forms of human organization. According to Dr. Malcolm Klein, the former director of the Social Science Research Institute at the University of Southern California, a street gang is durable in that it remains stable even

---

[6] Monica Davey, "In a Soaring Homicide Rate, a Deep Divide in Chicago," NYT, A1-A14, January 3, 2013.

with significant and frequent member turnover; it is public in that the group spends time in public spaces (like the street) or makes an effort to promote its image in a public way; its members are young — most participants in gang culture are teenagers or are in their twenties (though the age cap is flexible); it is involved in illegal behavior of some kind; and it has a discrete identity that it is proud of and makes an effort to promote. Of course, the line between a street gang and a more highly organized criminal syndicate can be blurry — sometimes street gangs, prison gangs, and mafia-like organizations engage in a degree of cooperation. An individual gang may also be an element of a particular political or social justice movement.[7]

Humans are very social. We have families, social groups and communities. But those units have been shrinking. People talk about isolation. Everyone tries or is encouraged to organize and collaborate with others. We all want to belong to something, but what?

Most of our information and opinions about gangs come from movies and television series about mob bosses, prohibition gangsters and drug lords from the 1920s and later. Names like Al Capone, Bugsy Siegel and others come to mind as do movies like *Scarface*. These are narratives compiled out of contemporary portraits that create a larger meta-narrative of our culture.

---

[7] "18 with a bullet, Gang Violence Around the World," http://www.pbs.org/wnet/wideangle/episodes/18-with-a-bullet/gang-violence-around-the-world/1392/.

The first academic and widely cited study of gangs was published in 1927. The book was a sociological study of the thousands of gangs in Chicago.[8] Who joins a gang? Mostly young men who are minorities, but women are now joining in increasing numbers.

> The Chicago Crime Commission estimated that females accounted for as many as 20,000 of the 100,000 gang members in the city at the turn of the century. In the past, girls and young women often occupied, or appeared to occupy, somewhat subservient roles within gangs. A study conducted in the late 1990s revealed, however, that increasing numbers of females were becoming full-fledged gang members and increasingly participating in gang-related violence.[9]

Gangs break down into racial and ethnic groups, using culture to establish community.[10] Gangs and community organizations in the 1960s and earlier are discussed in more than one source on the subject. Venkatesh quoted the following: "'You need to understand that the Black Kings are not a *gang*; we are a *community organization*, responding to people's needs.'"[11] But their business is selling drugs. "They rarely spoke openly about drugs, other than to note the death of a supplier or a change in the price of powder cocaine. Most of their talk concerned the burdens of management: how to keep the

---

[8] See Frederic Milton Trasher, *The Gang: a study of 1,313 gangs in Chicago*. Chicago, Ill: University of Chicago Press, 1927.
[9] Andrew J. Diamond, "Gangs," The Electronic Encyclopedia of Chicago, Chicago Historical Society, http://www.encyclopedia.chicagohistory.org/pages/497.html, 2005.
[10] Ibid.
[11] Sudhir Venkatesh, *Gang Leader For A Day, A Rogue Sociologist Takes to the Streets*, p. 186.

shorties in line, how to best bribe tenant leaders and police officers, which local businesses were willing to launder their cash."[12]

Why do people join a gang? They join for both what they perceive to be economic opportunity and for their community, but their fate and that of those whom they engage most often leaves them with "nought but grief an' pain."[13] Most gang members end up dead or in jail. According to Vankatesh, there is a "constant threat of arrest and imprisonment, injury and death."[14] And later in the same chapter Venkatesh quotes a member of the gang he got to know who told him you don't leave. "'If I leave the gang...will come after me and kill me. If I stay in the gang, the police will throw me in jail for thirty years. But that's the life...'"[15]

Starting in the late 1880s, waves of new immigrants became the new recruits for gangs formed by ethnic ties or as reactions to growing ethnic populations. This trend continues today. And as gang territory becomes less lucrative, disputed gangs break out into wars. In Chicago in 2012 the homicide rate was at a near record high as other crimes reached a

---

[12] Ibid., 187.
[13] Robert Burns, "To a Mouse, on Turning Her Up in Her Nest with the Plough," 1785, excerpt of original and translation, http://en.wikipedia.org/wiki/To_a_Mouse.
[14] Ibid., 188.
[15] Ibid., 190.

30 year low.[16] Davey notes, "With the city's longtime gangs splintering into fractions and increasing problems with retaliatory violence, homicides rose suddenly..."[17]

The exhibition, *Art Engaging Gangs*, does not contain images of bloodshed. The works engage cultural, social and economic issues relating to gangs. It includes art in different media that loosely make reference to different artistic movements, including styles and periods from Dutch Genre to Ash Can School to German Realism to Pop art.[18] The exhibition does not analyze or categorize these works by "isms" that they might fall into, but there are some historical periods that will be lightly referenced.[19]

These are not the first group of artists to use imagery that references political, social and cultural issues.[20] Dutch Genre artists referenced domestic scenes, creating paintings that reveal moral lessons for the viewer. The works act as a visual Protestant Bible and portraits that have come down to us of the people who lived then. For instance, in the

---

[16] Monica Davey, "In a Soaring Homicide Rate, a Deep Divide in Chicago," NYT, A1-A14, January 3, 2013.

[17] Ibid.

[18] The scope of this paper greatly limits any detailed discussion of these references.

[19] There is not enough time and distance to place this work historically. As for some of the early history the following should be considered. "'German Realism of the Twenties: The Artist as Social Critic," deals with successor of Expressionism in Weimar Germany. After World War I, the inner-directed art of the Expressionists and their belief that art had the ability to transform both individuals and the community could no longer withstand the daily chaos of life. Artists such as George Grosz and Otto Dix made disturbing and at times grotesque pictures to assail the hypocrisy of the bourgeois establishment. This is a noteworthy episode in the history of modern art when, for a brief time, a close interweave between art and politics existed, and the socio-economic situation acted as a catalyst for the production of compelling works of political art." Peter Selz, *Beyond the Mainstream*, Cambridge, Cambridge University Press, 1997, p.s. 4-5.

Lace Maker (1662), a painting by Dutch artist Caspar Netscher, the artist depicts a young girl sitting quietly by herself making lace. There are two empty shells near her on the floor. This is an image of a poor but a hardworking and moral girl who eats shell fish that she has gathered as she works. There are many other examples of paintings that depict images of domestic virtue. On the other hand, depictions of a woman reading a love letter or playing an instrument implies something more; the images meant more to contemporary viewers than a lovely depiction of a woman at rest in her home. The morality of the subject is ambiguous. Is the letter from her husband? Or her lover? Contemporary viewers would have understood the painting as depicting a woman reading a letter from her lover while her husband was away. Compare this theme to contemporary portrayals of New York in the luminescent paintings by the Hudson River School. The paintings are beautiful landscapes with shimmering light. The Hudson River is still there. Later the Ash Can School captured a different landscape of NYC. While on the whole the art does portray the life of the immigrant, the glasses are still rosier than reality. In contrast, Goya's *Third of May* is not rosy. It depicts a violent and visible execution of Spanish fighters by the French under Napoleon in the early 1800s. It is a depiction of war, violence and death.

---

[20] A thorough analysis of the references to early art is beyond the scope of this paper as is all the differences of the artists in this exhibition to earlier artists whose are engaged social political issues.

German Expressionism was followed later by German Realism and later after Abstract Expressionism in the 1960s, by Pop artists who all took up political and cultural issues.[21] There are many examples in art history where artists have acted as a social critic through their work.[22] The group of artists shown here is not new to the practice. What is different is that while other work comments on governments, corporations, museum boards and wars, the art here acts as intimate domestic portraiture.

This themed exhibition is the flip side of Norman Rockwell's paintings of Thanksgiving gatherings in Middle America or getting immunized, a shot, from the doctor to protect you from unseen danger. The artwork shows a different kind of danger: the danger of poverty, lack of work and opportunity. The work reflects and documents the violence and death that surrounds the lives of gang members and victims. It is also the sea we swim in through mass media; we might be aware of a shift in the current, but not the water any more. "...the neighbor who might have yelled at the misbehaving teenager in the old days was less likely to do so, since that kid might well be carrying a gun."[23] Gangs not only sell drugs to anyone and everyone, they extort money from anyone they can. They argue that they are taking care of the communities because the rest of society is not

---

[21] See Peter Selz, *Art of Engagement*. Berkeley: University of California Press, 2006.
[22] Discussion of the artists and movements in any detail are beyond the scope of this paper.
[23] Sudhir Venkatesh, *Gang Leader For A Day, A Rogue Sociologist Takes to the Streets*. New York: The Penguin Press, 2008, p. 61.

taking care of them.   The poor are generally invisible. They are the Other. We hope they are being helped and taken care of by the community. But, before a community the more basic group is your family.

Children learn from their parents to be careful when crossing the street.   A parent teaches them to look both ways before crossing the street and not to talk to strangers. In a parental example of teaching a child about their environment, or their community, artist Joseph Rodriguez photographed a black and white snapshot, a portrait of a family in his 1993 series *East Side Stories* included in this exhibition. It is a simple but very powerful photograph of a father with his little girl. He is showing his daughter a handgun.   A mother is standing, smiling, in the background. It would be a very warm and domestic scene if it were not for the gun and bullets on the floor. Does she play with them? Are these her toys? It seems that way. Instead of a doll to play with the little girl has a gun and bullets. These are the tools that she will need to defend herself in her community. This young girl is learning her lessons, learning how to handle an instrument in her home. This is not a music lesson that is portrayed here. We are taken aback by the scene and we should be. But why? Parents have a duty to protect their children. Shouldn't he teach his child to protect herself? Or maybe she just hears gun shots at night in her neighborhood and he is showing her what makes those noises. He has a gun himself and like the child of a baker or candlestick maker he is sharing with his daughter.   The image is stronger because it is a girl and a father and not a little boy and a father. If he was showing a gun and bullets to a little boy would our reaction be different? Probably, but it shouldn't be. In too many neighborhoods this is how you take care of yourself.

Another of Rodriguez's photographs in this exhibition shows a young man counting his money. He's not a bank teller. The implication is that these are the proceeds from drug sales or have been taken from others for his "protection." Other images in this series show young men pointing a gun at the viewer and at each other. All are black and white, styled as simple snapshots of residents in the neighborhood. But, the photos portray the Other in black and white, almost ghosts that we try to ignore, but cannot. These images do not show Mister Rogers's neighborhood or Sesame Street. Color would be distracting and his message would be lost.[24]

Several of the artists in this exhibition use portraiture to display a captured domestic moment. In Rodriquez's photographs, the moment is in the future, but probably not too far into the future. What will happen in the next moment or the next week? Someone will shoot that gun and someone will probably die. Maayke Schurer's video also seems playful, acting as a simple portrait of young men goofing around and showing off. It is a moment both contemporary and, in retrospect, foreshadowing the fate of the young

---

[24] Joseph Rodreguez's book of photograph's *East Side Stories,* 1992 is available for viewing as part of this exhibition. Rodríguez, Joseph, Rubén Martínez, and Luis J. Rodriguez. 1998. *East Side stories: gang life in East L.A.* New York: PowerHouse Books.

participants; less than a month later one of the young rappers was stabbed to death. The living moments in Robert Taub's portraits are gone. They reveal an existence cut short, acting as portraits of the dead who will never know a full life. This is also true of Throwell's portraits of his father, adapted from family snapshots.

Nadín Ospina plays with memories from our childhood. Ospina repurposes toys and popular figures such as Mickey Mouse and Bart Simpson. In his video, *Colombialand*,[25] Lego figures act out the drama of farming a cash crop in the international capitalistic market. Farming what? Poppies that turn from red to gold. It's about growing and protecting your crop at all costs. It's about drug trafficking in the Americas. The figures that populate the video are not real. The land is first overlaid with green Lego blocks, a transformation representing the symbolic control and power of international forces that are taking over the land. These Legos may seem like just plastic toys, but they are much more. The Legos are interlinking plastic blocks, mass produced and commercially available worldwide. The plastic constructs were all supplied by an international corporation. They represent the un-natural and the artificial. Everyone and everything is built out of the same blocks. Identity is constructed from the outside. These are portraits not of individuals, but of people who have become cogs in the international machine.

---

[25] Originally exhibited in Instituto Cervantes de París. Cervantes, Paris, 2007 as part of a larger installation. Ospina, Nadín. 2007. *Colombialand.*

They grow this crop that is death. Ospina's appropriation of this toy, this building block, is appropriate to the subject. Cultures collide in Ospina's work. Ospina has built a Lego community of a toy farmer with his wife and child, soon joined by a man in a military uniform with a very large gun. One figure who might have complained is in chains. There are sounds of chaos, but things go on as they were. More fields, more red poppies sprout up. It all ends with an image of a grinning skeleton. The themes are Death and violence, but there is no blood. It is supposed to be bloodless. It all just seems like playtime, but it's not; it is a business.

Ospina is known for his complex combinations of Pop culture imagery with ancient pre-Colombian forms. His work questions the formation of our identity in the modern mass media world. This is not Ospina's first work that integrates drug culture/Pop culture into large sculptures. *Principe de las flores* (2002), a very large outdoor sculpture of Mickey Mouse, was exhibited in Madrid. In Ospina's statement about the work he argues that the sculpture is "based on the Aztec sculpture Xochipilli found in Tlamanalco, Mexico. This image is covered with representations of psycho tropical plants (Peyote, Datura, Borrachero, Yajé). It is a critical reference to the ancient ritual consumption and the pathological contemporary consumption of drugs. You know that it is a very sensitive topic for me as a Colombian."[26] *Colombialand* shows the beginning of the drug trail. The trail ends with gang members who turn powder cocaine into crack in a kitchen. The crack is then put into small little plastic packets. Then little packets are delivered for sale.[27] While it all seems domestic, it is very uniform for what might look like a mom and pop operation, in reality it is an international franchise business. Like candy processed from cocoa beans and vanilla into a small piece of chocolate, this process creates a product that is more addictive. It all seems so simple and sweet.

Sweet and childlike is a feeling also evoked in Robert Taub's larger than life and full of life paintings from his series *Resurrection Cemetery* (2005-2006). The person depicted, however, is dead. Their portrait consists of the person's gravestone and the detritus left by the grieving. Friends and relatives bring toys to the graves in an effort to comfort themselves, or, perhaps in the hope of resurrection, allowing their dead child or friend to take their favorite toy to the next life. Taub's paintings are based on rubbings that the artist made from gravestones in East Los Angeles, featured in this exhibition, with multiple images from many gravestones painted on a very large canvas. Each subject's life was short. They were gang members.

---

[26] Email from Ospina cited in Holly Crawford, *Attached to the Mouse, Disney and Contemporary Art.* Maryland: University Press of America, 2006, 189.
[27] Venkatesh, Gang Leader for a Day, 109.

These are portraits of people taken in their new home--the cemetery and grave site. They don't seem to be just a name on a gravestone, but they are. We know very little about them. "...they remain anonymous even in death, their identity reduced to a name—an abstract, a commonplace signifier remembered only by their families."[28] Taub's work is also a *memento mori*, Donald Kuspit argues about the series of grave side rubbings.[29] Why would Taub make a *memento mori* to fallen gang members? It seems Taub was a gang member earlier in his life.[30] His portraits are of the fallen whom he might have known. They completed the path he did not take. Kuspit comments that Taub's earlier rubbings seem to be "in permanent mourning..."[31] The same could be said of the larger paintings, even though they are colorful. Instead of a small reminder of death and the path that Taub did not take, these are larger than life. They look like small movie billboards of a movie cut short discarded on the editing room floor. What was their narrative? The large scale calls out to the viewer, but is ultimately silent. As Kuspit points out, the painting "suggests who they [the subject] have killed –themselves."[32] And it is children who are being recruited into gangs as Taub's painting so painfully remind us,

[28] Donald Kuspit, essay in Robert Taub, *Resurrection Cemetery, Life and Death in East LA and earlier work*. monograph, 2001, p. 3.
[29] Ibid., 3.
[30] Ibid., 4.
[31] Ibid., 3.
[32] Ibid., 3.

"while others prosper."[33] In his essay in Taub's monograph Kuspit writes, "What is extraordinary is Taub's engagement and determination: his project shows that art is welcome where nothing else is, and healing where nothing else can be. Taub in effect became the community's shaman, a kind of artist-priest dealing constructively with the tragedy that the community's official priest tried to prevent, but could not."[34]

Taub's paintings beautifully show us name after name of the youths who took all the risks and lost. So who is winning and why were they, the victims, sucked in to this life? A gang acts as your community and your path, your hope for the "good" life. Members hope to move up the ranks and make the big money. A gang's structure, according to Venkatesh, mirrors any large corporation.[35] Their business is selling drugs and other activities that go beyond what most of us would identify as community organization. "The poorest parts of the city were controlled largely by street gangs like the Black Kings, which made their money not only dealing drugs but also by extortion, gambling, prostitution, selling stolen property, and countless other schemes. It was outlaw capitalism…netting small fortunes for the bosses…"[36] But, what the rest of the community really gets is "drug addiction and public violence…"[37] The bottom tiers of the gang take all the risks for very little return. A

---

[33] Sudhir Venkatesh, *Gang Leader For A Day,* p. 35.
[34] Donald Kuspit, essay in Robert Taub, p. 4.
[35] Venkatesh, *Gang Leader For A Day*, 35.
[36] Ibid., 37.
[37] Ibid.

gang leader on the street only makes $30,000 a year.[38] The younger men that work for him make far less, some holding jobs washing cars and working at McDonalds.[39]

The KKK fits into this model of community organizers, even though we regret their methods and the community they were working so hard to preserve.[40] Yes, the KKK originally argued that they served as community organizers and protectors.[41] "In an era without Social Security or widely available life insurance, men joined fraternal organizations such as the Elks or the Woodmen of the World to provide for their families in case they died or were unable to work. The founder of the new Klan, William J. Simmons, was a member of twelve different fraternal organizations. He recruited for the Klan with his chest covered with fraternal badges, and consciously modeled the Klan after fraternal organizations."[42] The pointed hoods they wore allowed them to hide. Erik Bergrin creates shaped canvas sculptures using the recognizable, white, blank KKK hoods as a basis. He then constructs this works with different motifs. One is black and covered with spider webs and skulls. Another is covered in cigarette butts and the third with nails that appear to be hammered into the surface. He explains, "I made a series of Ku Klux Klan hoods based on different themes. The whole idea behind these hoods is that people

---

[38] Ibid., 35.
[39] Ibid., 192.
[40] https://en.wikipedia.org/wiki/Ku_Klux_Klan.
[41] Discussion from daughter of a KKK member and internet site on the Klan. https://en.wikipedia.org/wiki/Ku_Klux_Klan.
[42] Ibid.

hide behind masks because of being in pain."[43] Bergrin takes control of the object and dilutes its power. He turns what we read as being part of the American history of racism, oppression and death into a series of masks that are used to strip the KKK of their own masks and power. His artwork unmasks the mask by re-purposing the symbol that signifies power through violence, secrecy and oppression of "others."

Mark Dillon also re-purposes material in his art. The material Dillon uses in his video, *Absence of Mind/"Get the Fuck Away From Me"* was very personal to him, as the grave sites are to Taub. Dillon alters and re-purposes a video of himself captured on CCTV as part of his healing process. The footage shows that Dillon was a victim of a violent crime. The footage that he acquired from the British police CTTV surveillance is of Dillon being stabbed by gang members. Through his art, Dillon takes control of this horrific event in his life. Like Bergrin, he drains the event of its power to control him by controlling the memory of the event. It does not take over his life-he takes control.

Maayke Schurer's video is in a much lighter vein. She also took control of a difficult situation, using her cell phone to make a video of a personal event. Her video is of a group of drunken gang members in Scotland who accosted her on the street. She talks to them and makes this video during which the gang members sing and brag about their gang affiliation. While the footage has the quality of a wacked home video, the narrative

---

[43] Email from the artist.

not recorded is the death of the leader of this gang three weeks after the chance video encounter. He died because of a gang stabbing.

Zefrey Throwell recently created a series, *At last...rest* (2013), that allowed him to express his sorrow and to create a *memento mori* about his father who died seven years earlier from a meth habit.   On his website, Throwell discusses how personal these paintings are to him and why he made them. "The most dangerous drug in the world - crystal, crank, Tina, methamphetamine or more commonly known as meth. The epidemic of meth use that has infected the United States is now spreading to Europe and the rest of the world. Destroying the lives of individuals, families and communities, meth threatens to undo the very fabric of our world."[44] According to the DEA, meth has traditionally been produced and transported in the United States by motorcycle gangs and other small independent groups who have established a decades old family lineage in the trade.[45]

The paintings are ghostly grey images adapted from snap shots taken over the course of his father's life, but they are not completely drained of life. One, for instance, is his father's high school graduation picture. It a standard head shot and could be of just about any senior in a tux, smiling about starting their life. The paintings act as a visual diary or scrapbook of the person his father will became. All of the paintings are portraits of a man

---

[44] Zefrey Throwell, http://www.zefrey.com/project_devils_bed.html.
[45] https://www.fas.org/irp/agency/doj/dea/product/meth/production.htm.

whose life has been written, and like Taub's paintings, these images are more for the living than about the dead. The soft images are familiar snap portraits, but they're ghoulish not because his father is dead but because the pigment Throwell uses to paint his very personal family portraits are his father's cremated meth laced ashes. Throwell comments that, "The remains still contain traces of meth which serve as both a deadly warning to those still living and a deeply personal memorial to a father who has passed on."[46] What he did is a taboo. We are supposed to bury the negative narratives with the dead. We are not supposed to air our dirty linen in public, especially not if they are ashes. This is an even bigger taboo. We are supposed to place human ashes in a pretty urn or sprinkle the remains of our loved ones into the ocean, not use them to make art. But Throwell did. In doing so, he mirrors what Taub, Dillon and Schurer did in their work, taking control of a very personal and sad narrative and he is making a new narrative for himself and anyone who cares to listen.

Two of the artists in this exhibition take a more objective and research approach to their art. They are creating archives. Historians spend their time in archives looking through letters, diaries, photographs and other material to sort out history. Have you ever asked how such material ended up in an archive? Who creates the archive that will ultimately affect how the meta-narrative is constructed? What is collected and what is saved? Is it

---

[46] Zefrey Throwell, http://www.zefrey.com/project_devils_bed.html.

all about kings, queens, presidents and captains of industry? That is one narrative, but what about the narrative of everyone else? Do they become no more than a name in the phone book or census record? They had a story, but no voice. They are not more than all the names and dates that Taub collected. It is a dizzying list, but how do you make a larger narrative from the all the smaller pieces?

Jasmine Johnson's video, *Other People, Other Groups* (2012), is a construction of narratives. It is a collection of mini portraits that captures a group of people at an instance. The context of a larger meta-narrative was captured and recorded by the mass media. The media gives us one narrative and Johnson gives us another. Her video is an archive of many different people's experience as bystanders to the London riot that took place in the late summer of 2011. What we see is what can be interpreted as a rehearsal with the participants just off screen from the major event.[47] Johnson gives the people voices and tells us, through voice over technique, what they were doing and thinking during the London Riots. What the viewer see is a white background with one or more actors with minimal props. Here is a fragment of the audio that you hear as you watch two young people, one male and the other female, on the screen. "Two media types...working for the BBC...new show...documentary of social inequality...not concerned

---

[47] Jasmine Johnson, *Other People Other Groups*, (2013). Excerpt of narrative.

with the people around them....they hold their laptops a little closer when they see the gangs of youth."

Here are some basic facts about the riot and who rioted. "The four days of rioting, triggered by a fatal police shooting August 4 in north London's Tottenham neighborhood, were the worst civil disturbances to hit Britain since the 1980s. Five people were killed and scores of stores were looted and buildings burned in several cities, including London and Birmingham. The Ministry of Justice says more than 1,500 people have been arrested and have appeared in court to answer charges from the riots. Some 22 percent of them were aged 10 to 17, and 91 percent were male."[48] Mobile technology was used by the rioters. The event has been labelled "'BlackBerry riots' because people used mobile devices and social media to organize."[49]   The whys, who and wherefores of the riots are still being discussed. "The riots have generated significant ongoing debate among political, social and academic figures about the causes and context in which they happened. Attributions for the rioters' behavior include structural factors such as racism, classism, and economic decline, as well as cultural factors like criminality, hooliganism, breakdown of social morality, and gang culture."[50]

---

[48] *London Riots, 2011. Most Rioters Had Criminal Records.* http://www.huffingtonpost.com/2011/09/06/london-riots-2011_n_950047.html.
[49] http://en.wikipedia.org/wiki/2011_England_riots.
[50] Ibid.

Paula Roush is interested in photography in archives and specifically the issues that arise around the intersection of photographic archives and self-publishing and teaching. "Once open and accessible, the archive can become a terrain for biographical, fictive and provocative interventions that challenge what was formerly the safe terrain of the historical document."[51] One example of her work is the open archive that she has created from the photographs of other artists. Those photographs are re-purposed here into small, self-published books of photographs taken by her students. Roush writes, "In a journey exploring what artists can do with archives, Anita Corbin's informal archive 'Invisible Girls' has been at the centre of an investigation into the photographic representation of contemporary youth cultures. It has been used to raise questions about the photograph as historical document and its archival status as a representation of the "other."[52] The materials presented in the small photographic books are portraits of girls that were taken in the 1980s. Who are they? How do their stories change when the context changes? These are some of the issues that Roush raises.

Her essay, *Download Fever: Photography, Subcultures and Online-Offline Counter-archival Strategies*, published in 2009 enumerates her concerns: "We ask questions about the photographic archive that are positioned at the intersection of three research areas. First,

---

[51] Paula Roush, "*Download Fever: Photography, Subcultures and Online-Offline Counter-archival Strategies.*" Essay in Photographies, Vol 2, no. 2 London: Routledge, 2009, p. 143.
[52] Ibid.

that of visual culture and its study, where the subject of youth culture appears as a contested field; second, the historical and institutional archival practices which contribute to the documentary status of the photograph together with new engagements with the archive in the form of the book and digital self-publishing practices; third, the teaching of photography in projects which involve archival art practices, and which explore situations and networks in Real Life and in Second Life."[53]

Photography before Photoshop was considered to be a record of facts, but all photographs are manipulated. Objects and people can be cropped from view when taking the image and afterwards by cutting the negatives. The factuality of the photograph falls apart with digital photography, but we still look at the image as fact. Why is this significant? We create our own personal narratives, and larger ones are created about our communities and culture. Humans create narratives when there are no facts to support them. Our minds want to make sense of the things we hear and see and put them into a neat box and close the lid. This archival lid is what Roush wants to open as an artist and educator. "The work developed in response to the box GS is a contribution to contemporary research on the meaning of archives for current artistic, educational and curatorial practices."[54]

[53] Paula Roush, "*Download Fever: Photography, Subcultures and Online-Offline Counter-archival Strategies,*" p. 154.
[54] Ibid., 163.

Restaurants come and go. Small businesses on any street corner are not, in this international economy, long lasting. Gangs also come and go "because it [is] unable to supply enough crack to meet the demand or because the gang leader sets his street dealers' wages too low to attract motivated workers."[55] But, it is all more than dollars and cents: it is lives.

But Mousie, thou art no thy lane,
In proving foresight may be vain:
The best-laid schemes o' mice an' men
Gang aft agley,
An' lea'e us nought but grief an' pain,
For promis'd joy!

(But little Mouse, you are not alone,
In proving foresight may be vain:
The best laid schemes of mice and men
Go often awry,
And leave us nothing but grief and pain,
For promised joy!) [56]

The schemes of young men who join gangs seem to come to "nought but grief an' pain…" They were the best laid plans of youth. Even though this stanza from Burns's poem uses the word in a different way than we would expect today, the overall meaning of this stanza, if not the entire poem, seems to be prophetic. The gang members' nests are torn

---

[55] Venkatesh, Gang Leader For A Day, 106.
[56] Robert Burns, "To a Mouse, on Turning Her Up in Her Nest with the Plough," 1785, excerpt of original and translation, http://en.wikipedia.org/wiki/To a_Mouse.

up. Projects were built and torn down for stadiums, conventions center, music centers and middle and high income homes for others in almost every major city.

We can walk quickly through this exhibition and the world around us, but we are just whistling past the grave yard. We think, "Not me. Oh no, not me. I'm not them. My neighborhood, my community, my life is different, it is not them." This is why we pay taxes and give money to charities. Society knows what to do. Do it. They will help. Do they? Can they? This essay and this exhibition pose more questions and have no answers, but they are important because the art engages the viewer and asks you to think about narratives and the courage it took each artist to take control of the narratives and events that were presented to them, creating art for us to ponder.

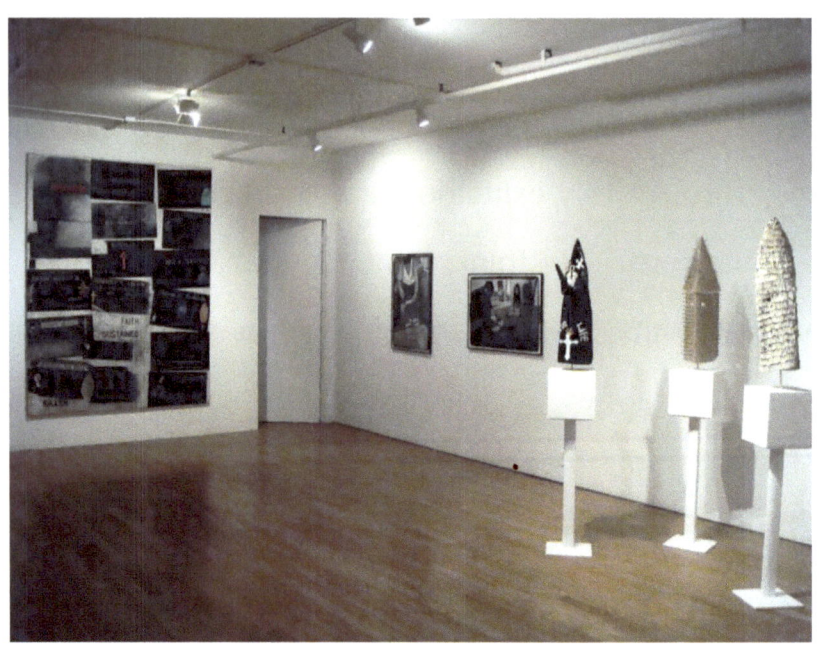

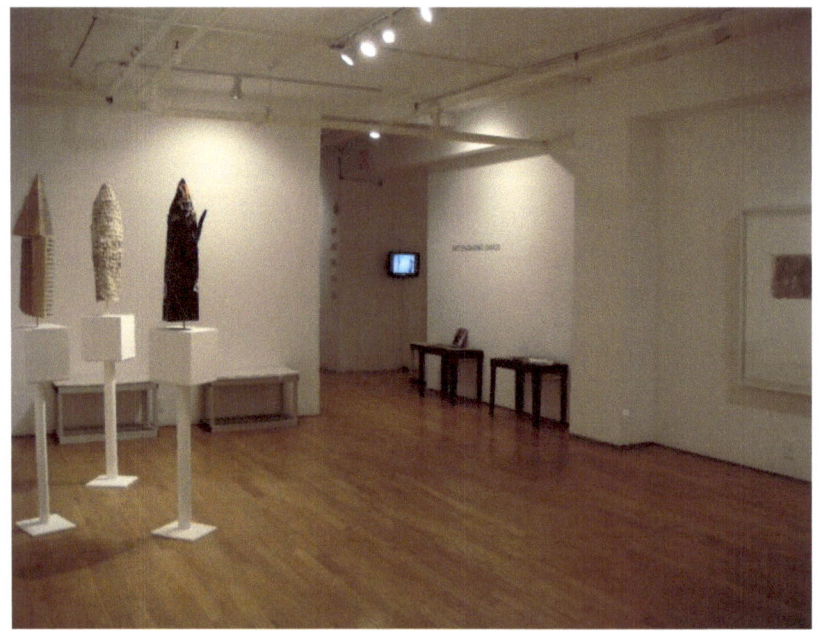

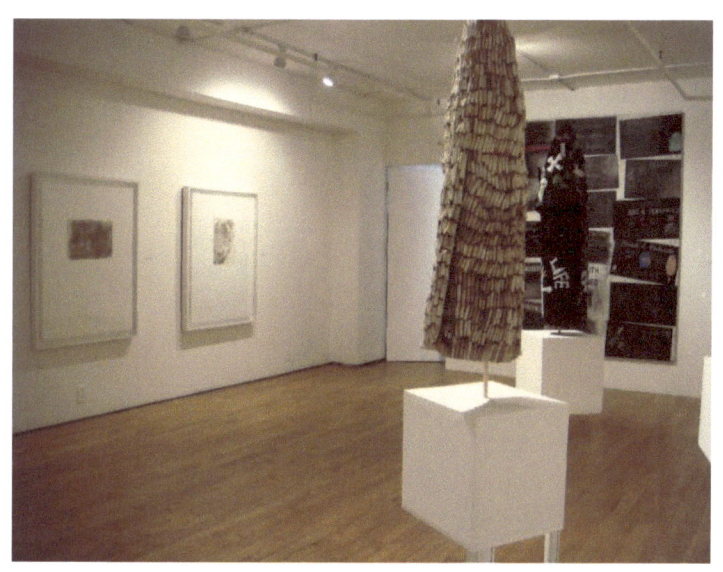

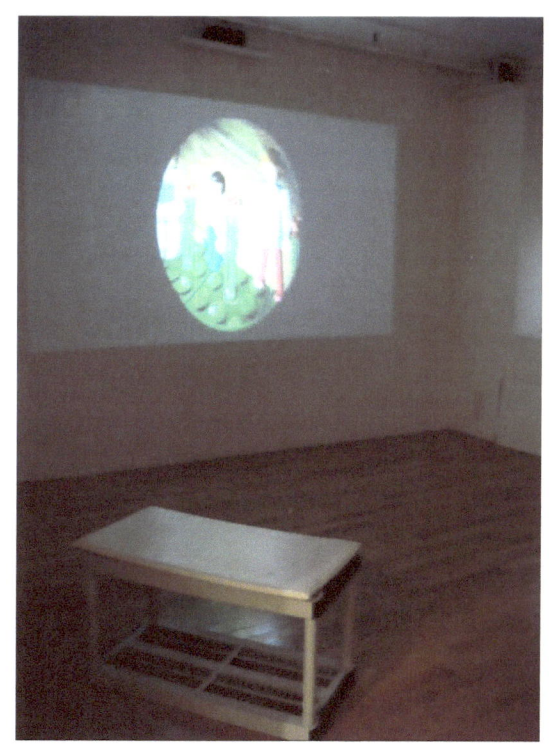

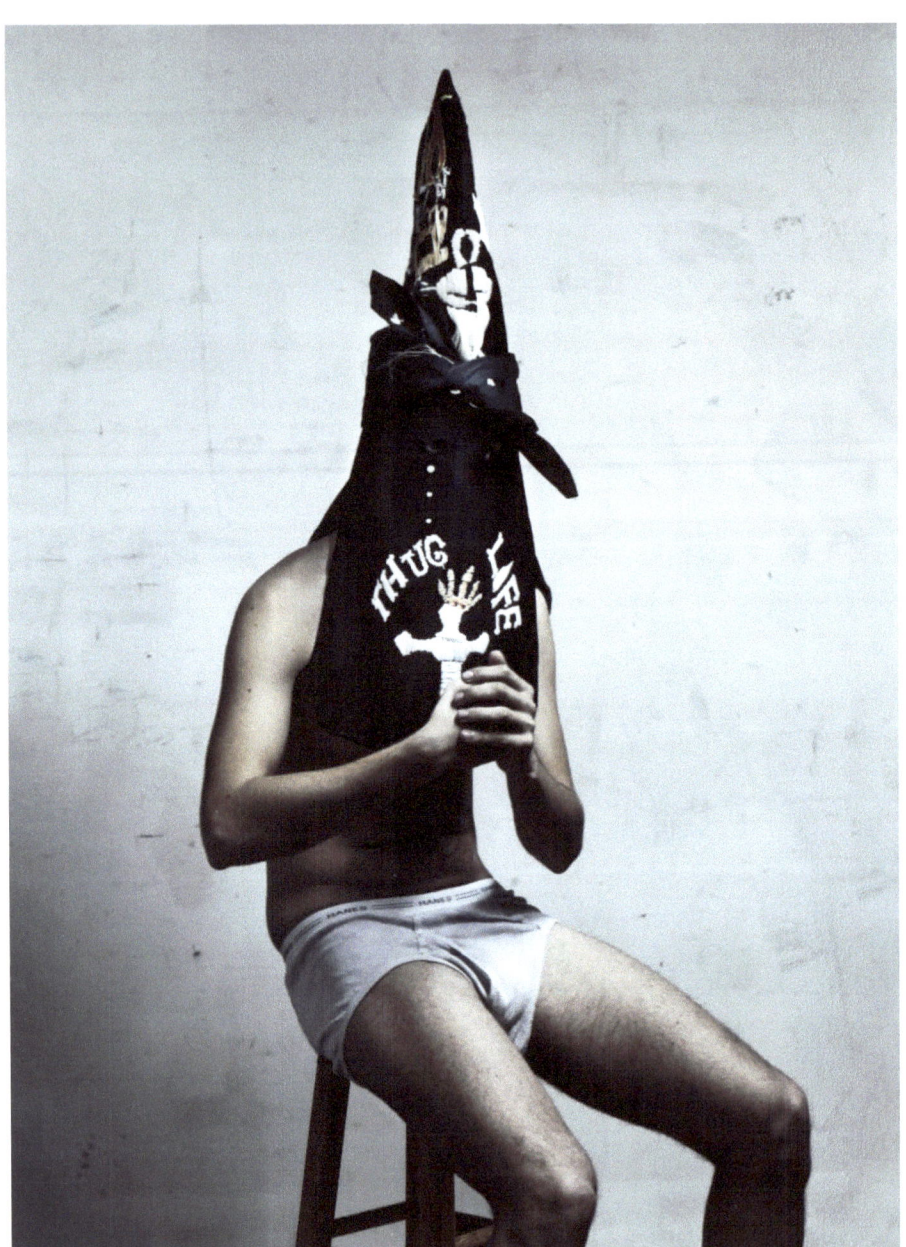

Erik Bergrin, *Gang KKK Hood*, 2012. Embroidered on cotton.

Erik Bergrin

KKK Hoods

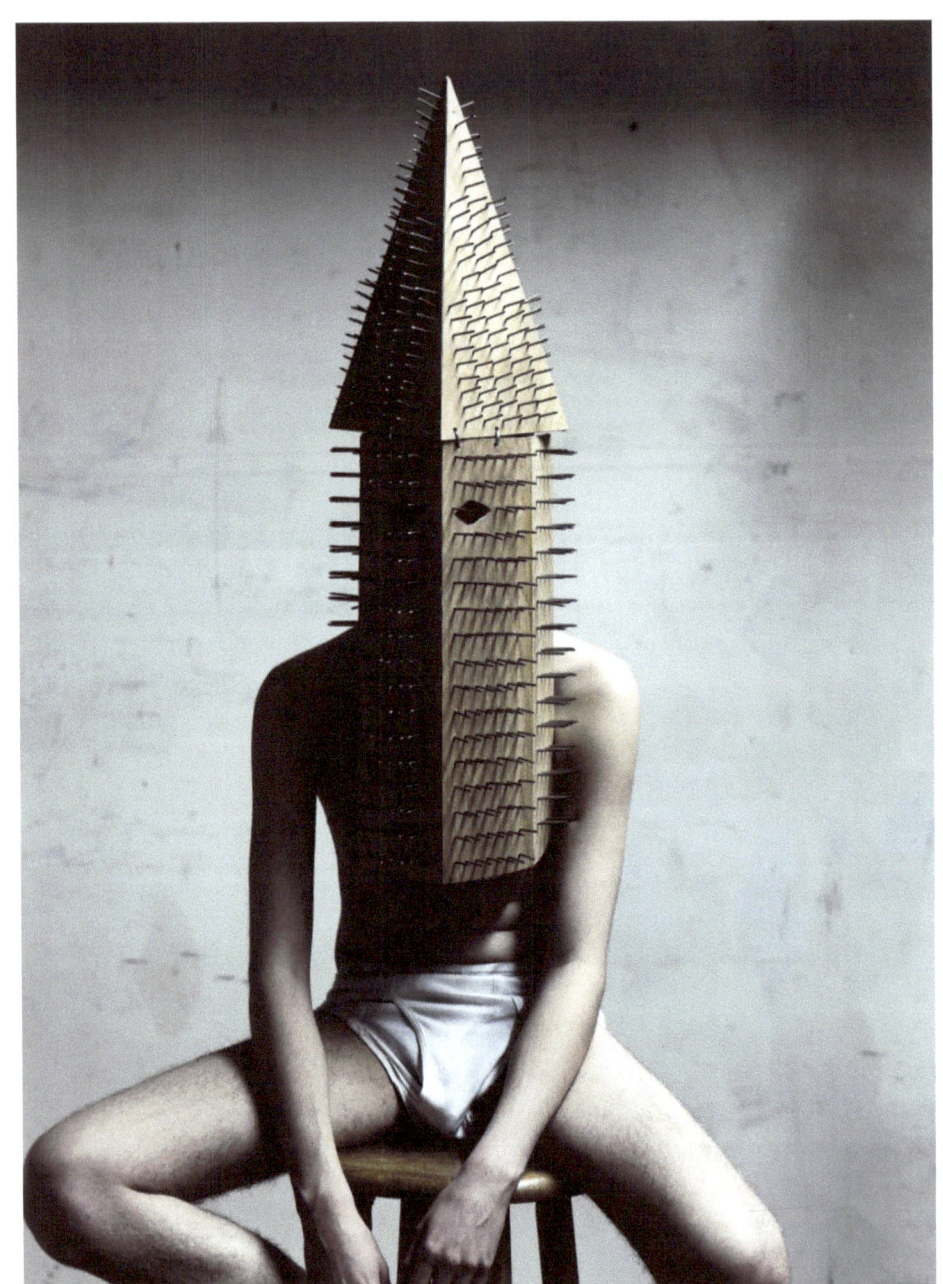

Wood and Nail KKK Hood, 2011. Wood, nails and wire.

KKK Hoods

I made a series of Ku Klux Klan hoods based on different themes. The whole idea behind these hoods is that people hide behind masks because they are in pain. My hoods deal with Identification within gangs via tattooing, over eating fast-food and so on. The hoods are manipulated to represent emotional damage. The embroidery is made up of hundreds and hundreds of needle punctures that represent pain. In this way, the KKK hoods draw a parallel between two evils.

-Erik Bergrin

Having studied psychology and clothing construction in school, Erik Bergrin left school feeling unfulfilled creatively. He was always making kooky costumes to go out in, and through this process developed a portfolio that landed him his first job creating puppets and team mascots for sports teams. From there he went on to another studio constructing historical replicas and clothing based costumes for Broadway and opera. With a very heavy influence in meditation, the ideas Erik tries to create are ones attempting to awaken the viewer and stop them from hiding from themselves. Erik utilizes repetitive motions in his creative process. His ideas stem from issues he wants to work out himself. He uses this repetitive action as a meditation to focus on the feeling he is running away from. Erik's work has been published in magazines such as WAD, Dazed and Confused, Ponytail, Schon, Zoo, Dust, The NY times, and Star magazine. He has shown in NY based galleries such as Place gallery, Niagra gallery, and Anomamous art salon. **www.erikbergrin.com**

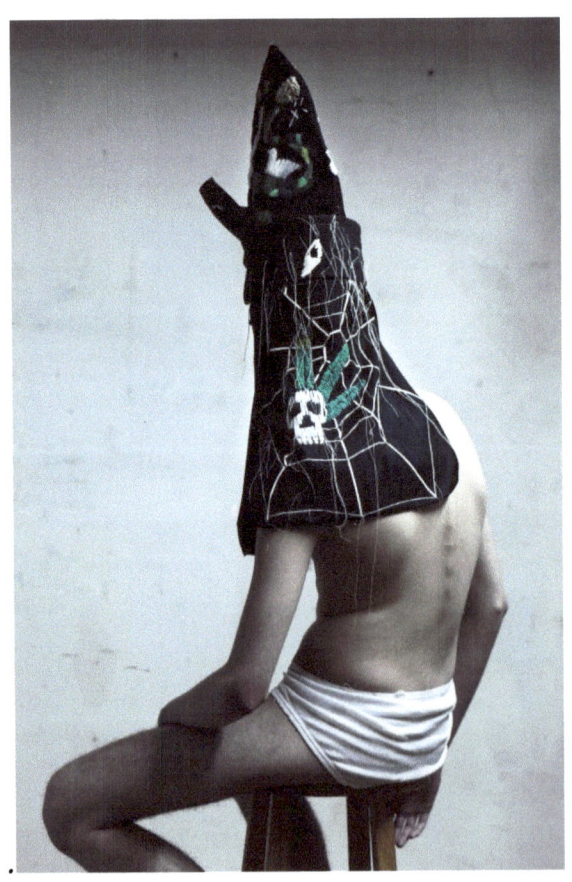

Gang KKK Hood, reverse.

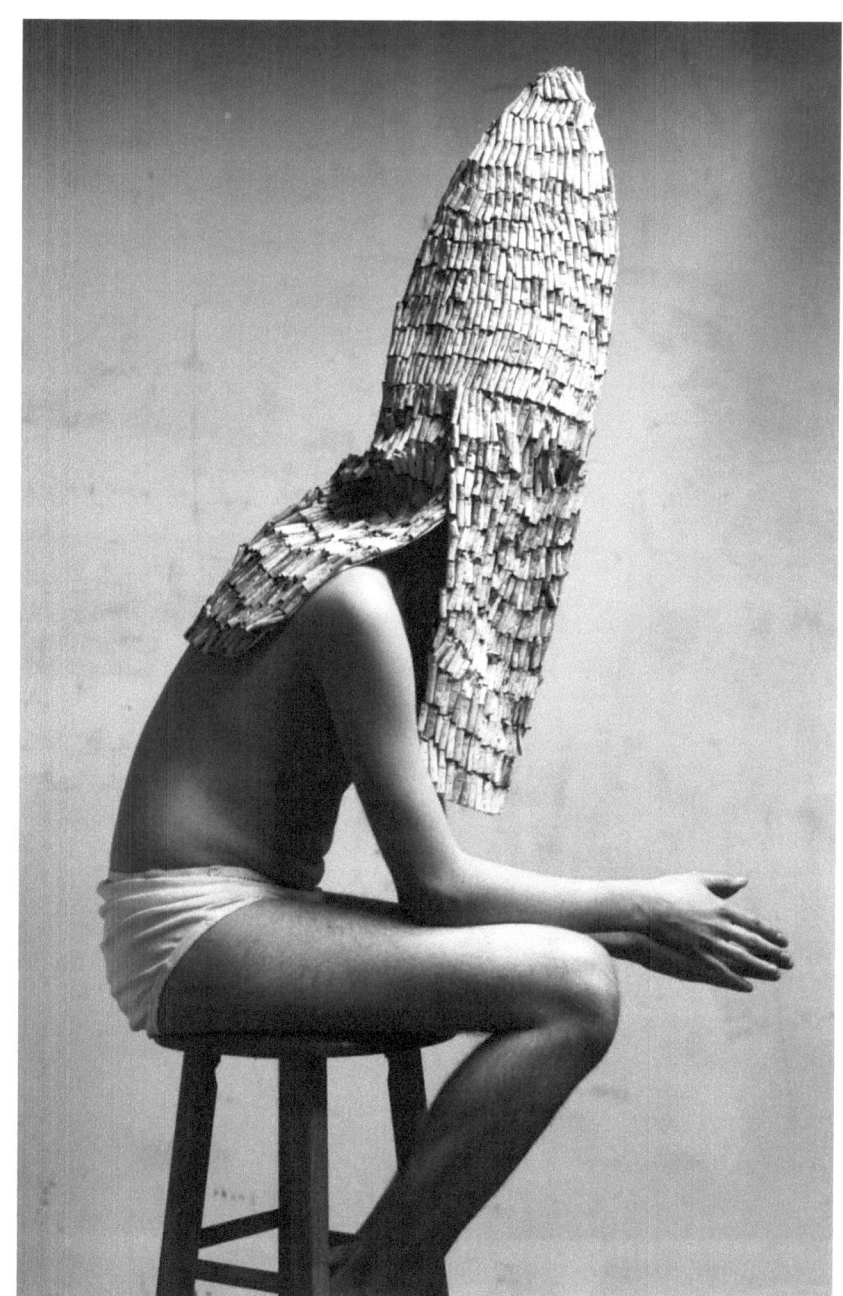

Cigarette Butt KKK Hood, 2011. Cotton and cigarettes.

• • •

35

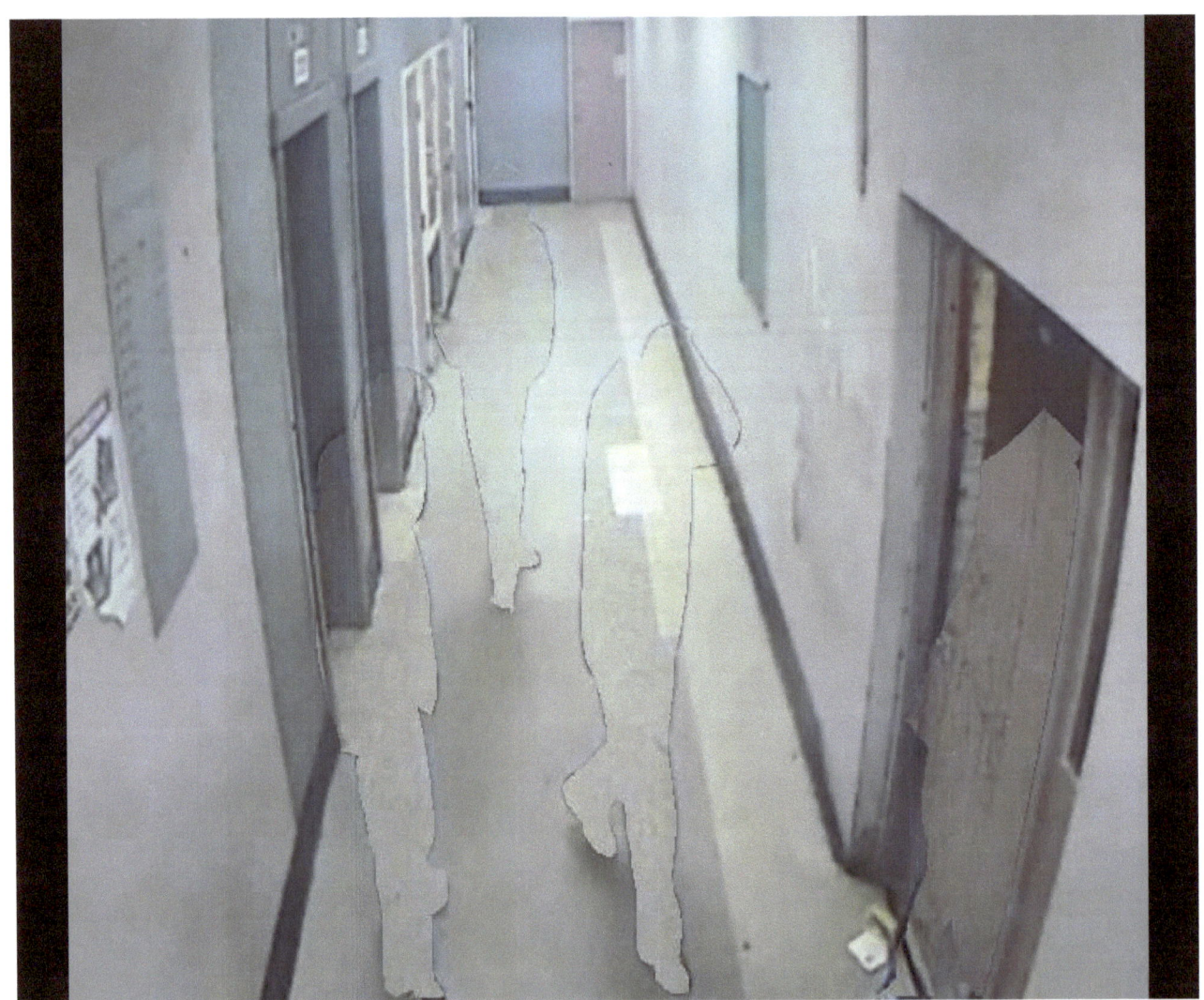

Mark Dillon, *Absence of Mind/"Get the Fuck Away From Me,"* 2013. Video, retrieved CCTV footage, subtitled with news articles, 14' 26." Video Still.

Mark Dillon

Absence of Mind/
"Get the Fuck Away From Me"

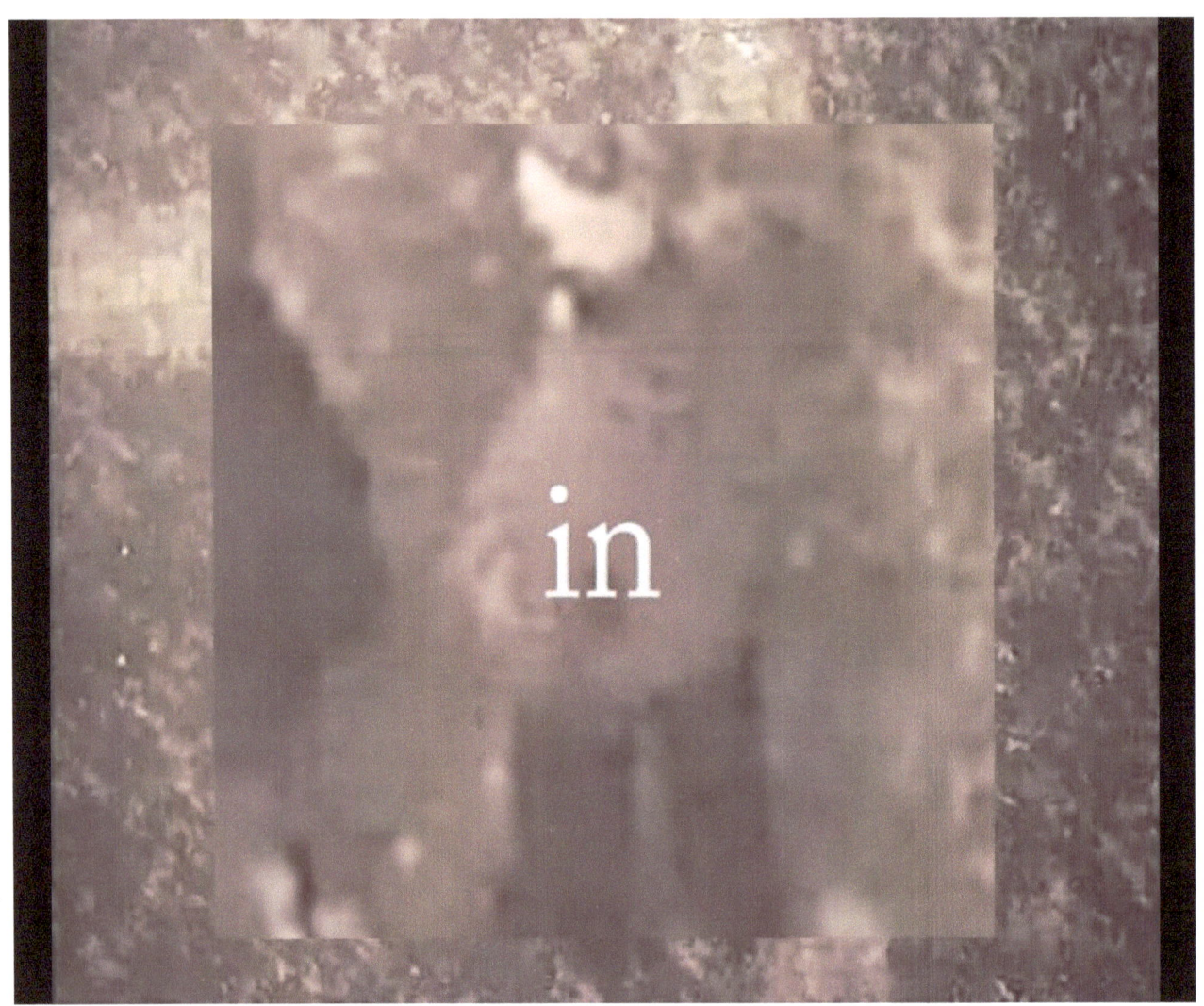

Absence of Mind/"Get the Fuck Away From Me," Video Still.

Absence of Mind/"Get the Fuck Away From Me"

Mark Dillon draws on elements of personal violent conflict as well as evidence of indirect brutality within the urban environment as a means of navigating and bringing reason to the tensions that form the cities we live in. The continual difficulty in understanding the rationale behind individual and social behaviour was born out of the constant analysis of retrieved CCTV footage leading up to the moment he was attacked. As a form of apparent objectivity that yields little concrete data, Dillon is left with a frustration towards a source material which is stubborn in its communication. The distance between subject and lens is something felt, and ultimately numbing for the viewer. A detachment that can be mirrored when justifying how a violent act can occur, a disconnection of consequence, a lack of empathy. In *Absence of Mind/"Get the Fuck Away From Me,"* 2013, the opening minutes present the viewer with CCTV scenes where subjects have been extracted, leaving only a slight evidence of their presence, a history, and creating a chasm between past and present. It also serves to focus on the surroundings of the figures, both in the interior/exterior architectures that provides the environment and also literally, within the images the shape of the silhouettes themselves. The absence of figures removes the importance of individual characteristics. The majority of the video is subtitled with news articles pertaining to the events unfolding. The content of the article removed from context and streamed word by word in such a manner serves to highlight the peculiarity of news media language. Its repetitiveness and apparent lack of depth in meaningful/experiential information is something Dillon found comparable to the study of his CCTV.

Mark Dillon was born in 1988 in London, UK. He completed his BA in Fine Art & Illustration at Coventry School of Art and Design, before completing an MFA in Fine Art Media at Slade School of Fine Art. Dillon has exhibited and held screenings across the UK and Ireland. As part of Present? Collective Dillon has recently shown at Maddox Arts (London) and taken up residency with CASK (Contemporary Art Society Kilcash, IRE). He has also shown regionally throughout the UK, including Brighton, Coventry, Luton and Stamford.

www.icwmarkdillon.com

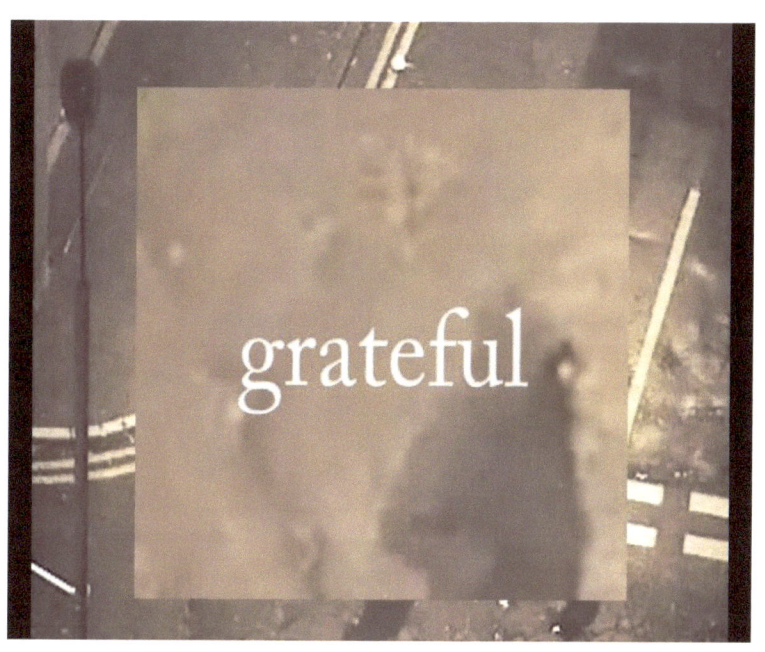

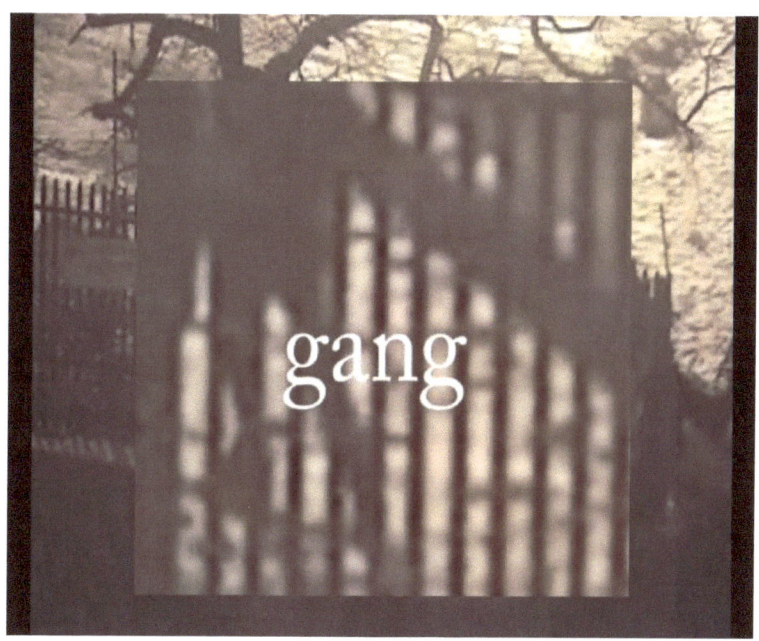

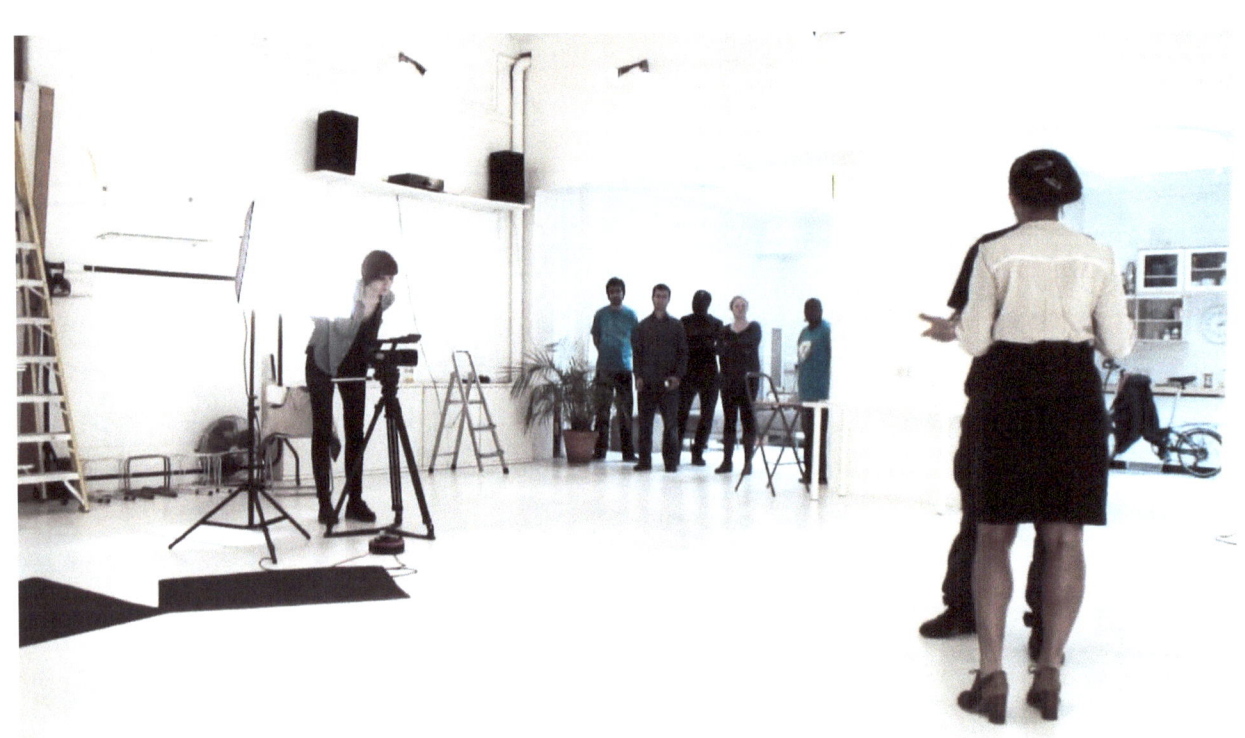

Jasmine Johnson, *Other People, Other Groups*, 2012. Video, 10'23". Video Still.

Jasmine Johnson

Other People, Other Groups

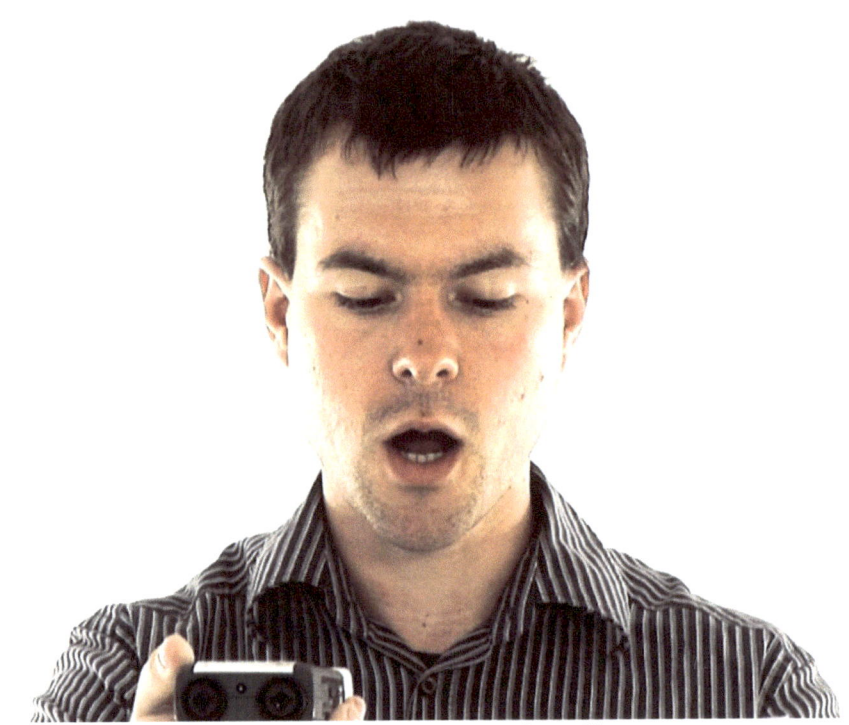

Other People, Other Groups, Video Still.

Other People, Other Groups

Other People, Other Groups utilises the studio in which Johnson re-makes 'experience' package pop videos for her freelance filmmaking as a site for a theatrical exercise 'The Dark Room' based on the theoretical work of director Augusto Boal. A group of eight cast one another into roles in the scenario (eg 'the bystander') and improvised characterisations, responding to a script based on James Meek's online article 'On Broadway Market,' written about a potentially violent situation and the leisure activities surrounding it. Participants included the artist, professional actors and members of Cardboard Citizens, a theatre group for homeless and displaced people who practice Boal's Forum Theatre.

Jasmine Johnson, b.1985, Brighton, lives and works in London.

Since graduating with a first from Nottingham Trent in 2007, Johnson has exhibited her work in London, England and Europe and staged her first solo show at AC Institute, New York in 2012. Group shows include Apriary Studio, London; Tether and Surface Gallery,

Nottingham, and the forthcoming Alumni Exhibition at Nottingham Trent University. She was selected for a two person DLR Public Arts Program commission to produce a film to mark the opening of the new station in Woolwich, South London. Presentations as part of the recently formed artist group MoreUtopia! include contributions to programmes at the Whitechapel Gallery and South London Gallery, both London, and a forthcoming symposium around Utopias this October in Rotterdam. She is currently studying towards her MFA at Goldsmiths, University of London.

She has recently returned from a group residency at Joya, Arte e Ecologia, Andalusia, Spain, in which she shadows Donna Beckman, who left Peckham to set up the eco resort, as she makes her own cheese. This forms part of a series of portraits of middle class women including Estelle Rogers who produces honey in her Herne Hill beehive, and Lesley McGuire, an actress and property developer who makes pesto as her son entertains himself in her contemporary Hackney kitchen. In Jasmine Johnson's videos and drawings the proximity of social groups and their lifestyles and aspirations collide, re-framing similarities and differences, often implicating the editorial control of the artist and provoking value judgements by the viewer with the effect of performing what Lauren Berlant terms 'intimate publics' in environments where the semi-staged both fictionalises and reaffirms archetypes. **www.jasmine-johnson.com**

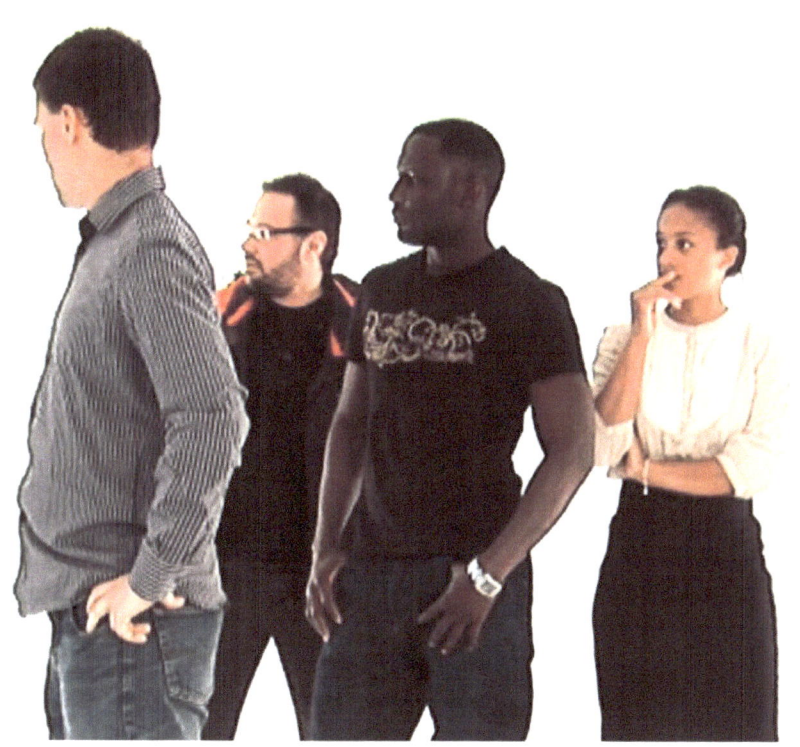

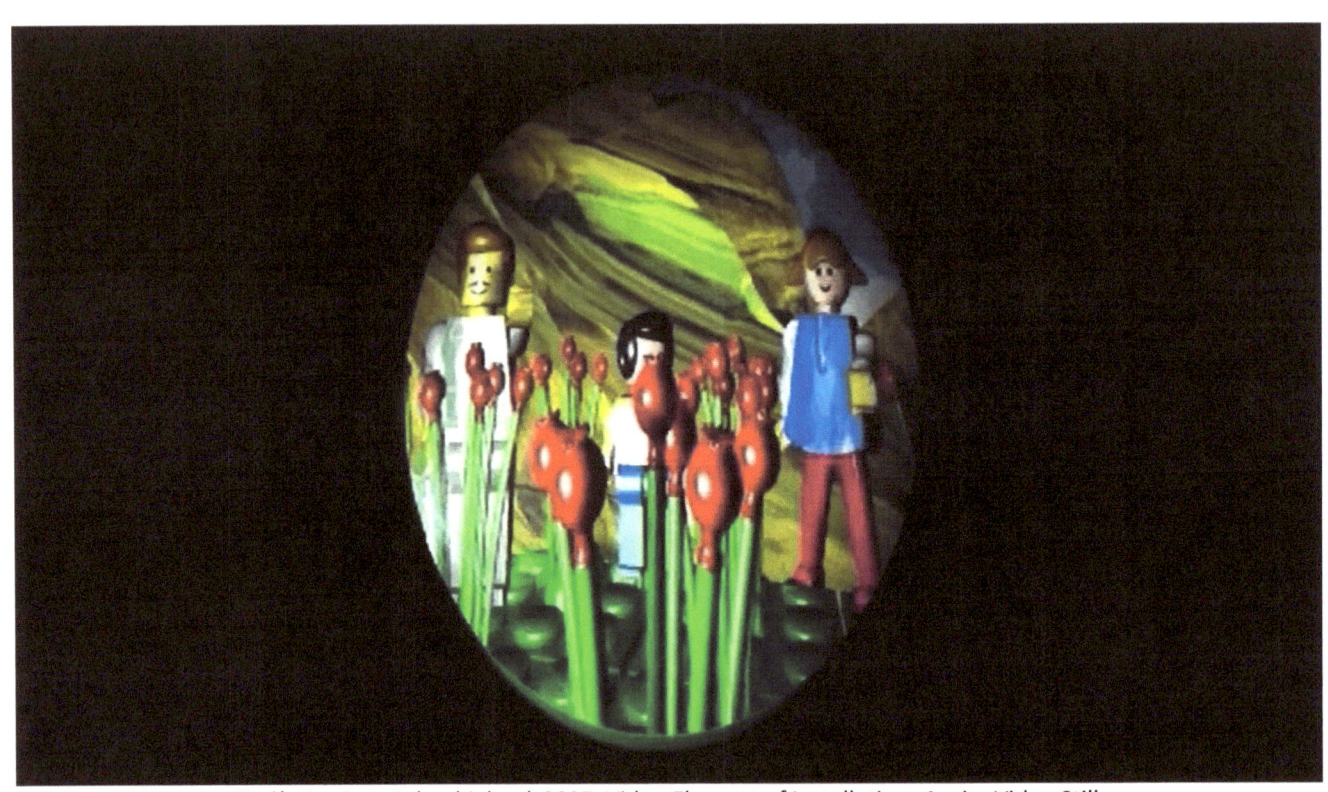

Nadín Ospina, *Colombialand*, 2007. Video Element of Installation, 4 min. Video Still.

Nadín Ospina

Colombialand

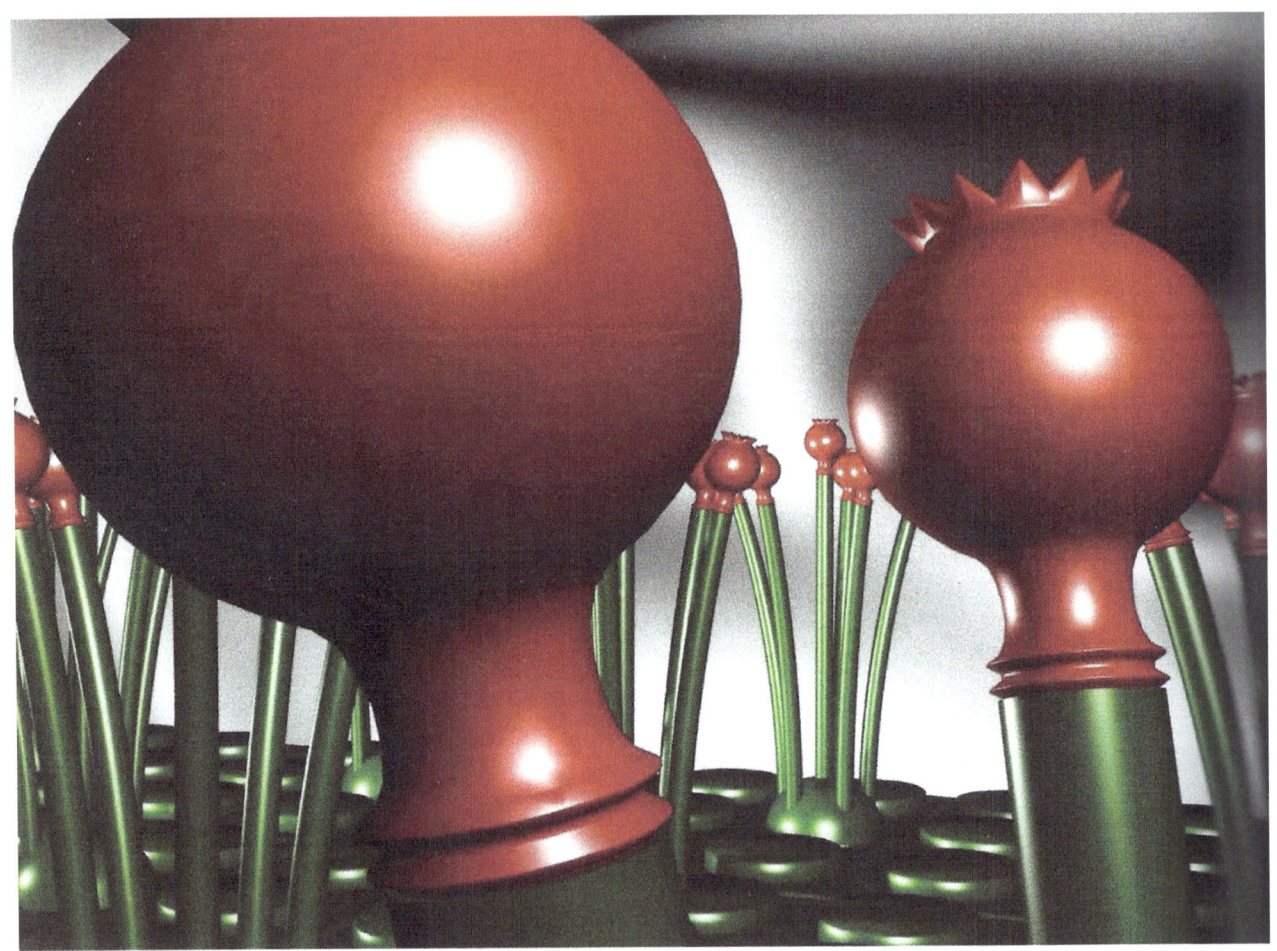

The Flowers of Evil 3, 2007. Oil on canvas, 130 x 160 cm.

Colombialand

This video element of *Colombialand* is a vision of the bloody and painful realities of Latin America expressed in images that appear to be of naive child's play. The 3DMAX animation gives the playful character of virtual reality to complex and real problems, questioning the manipulation of the media and the conduct of the company that has created these stereotypes in a game of mass local circulation.

- Nadín Ospina

Nadín Ospina (born May 16, 1960 in Bogotá, Colombia) is an award-winning Colombian artist with significant international exposure. His awards include First Prize, 34th Salon of Colombian Artists (1992) and First Prize, 18th Salon of Fire, Gilberto Alzate Avendaño Foundation (2004). From 1979 to 1982, he held the position of Professor of Fine Arts, Jorge Tadeo Lozano University in Bogotá. In 1992 he participated and is awarded at the Salón de Artistas Colombianos. In 1997, he was a John Simon Guggenheim Memorial Foundation Fellow in New York City. **www.nadinospina.com**

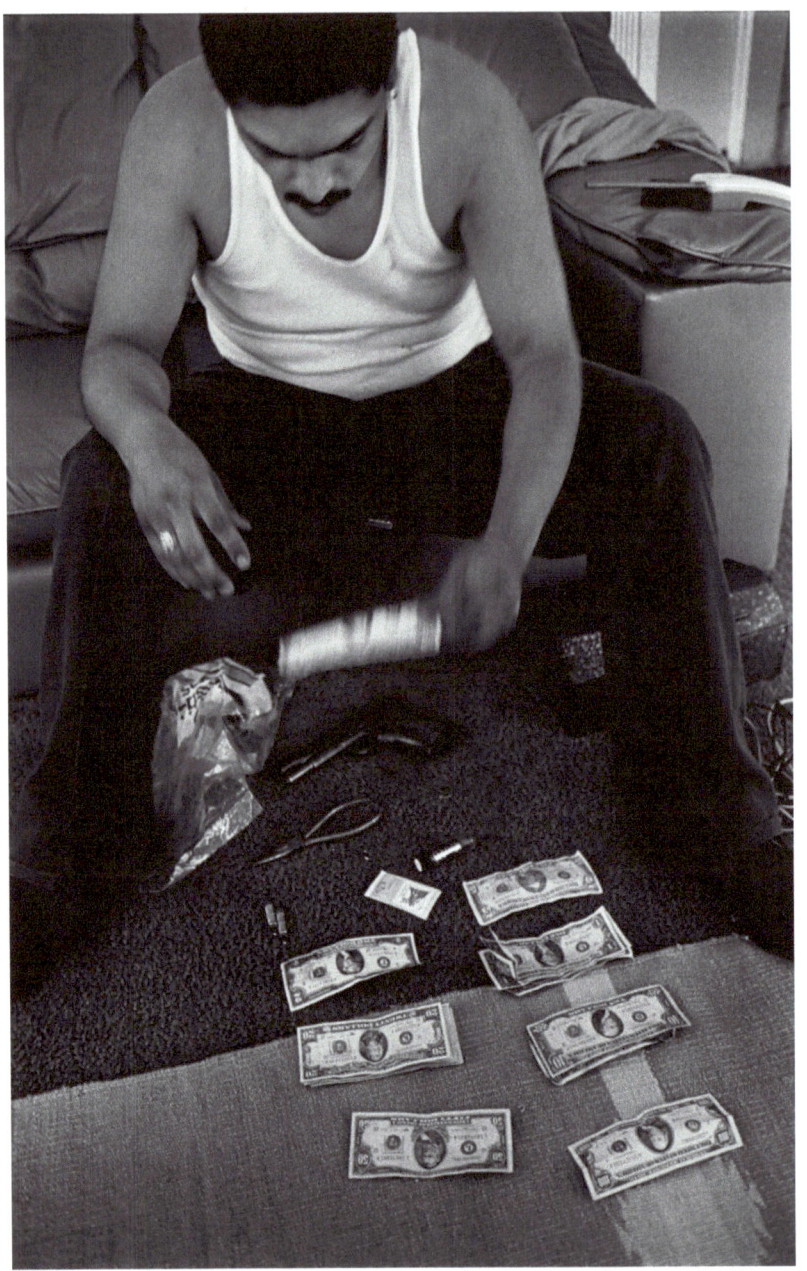

Joseph Rodriguez, *Chivo counts his money the morning after a carjacking,* 1993. Photograph.

Joseph Rodriguez

East Side Stories

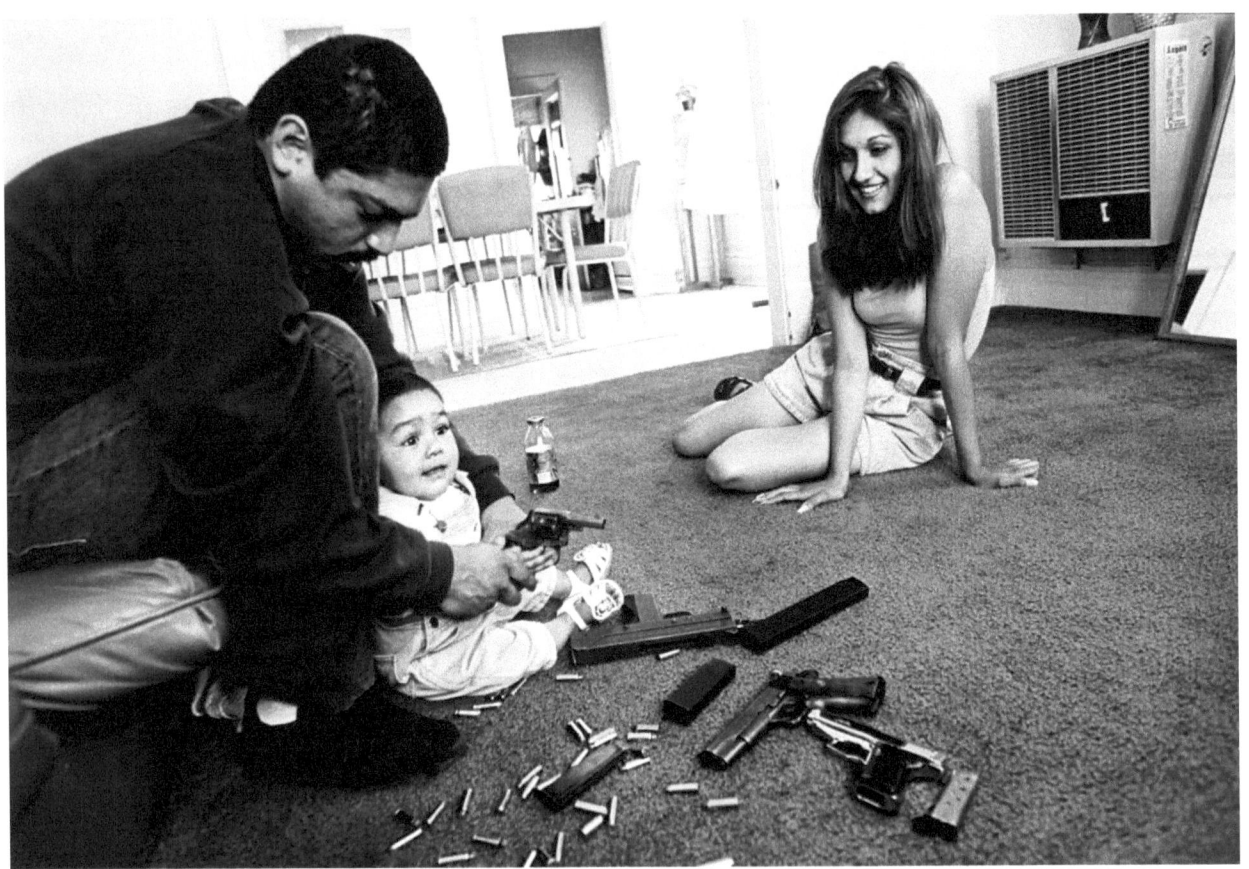

Joseph Rodriguez, *The morning after a rival gang tried to shoot Chivo for the fourth time. Chivo teaches his daughter how to hold a .32-caliber pistol. Her mother looks on. Boyle Heights,* 1993. Photograph.

East Side Stories

My interest in California began with street gangs in the early 1990s. Nearly two decades later, I continue photographing in California. My aim is to get to the core of violence in America, not just the physical violence against one another, but the quiet violence of letting families fall apart, the violence of unemployment, the violence of our educational system and the violence of segregation and isolation.

My work surges from both a profoundly personal and also a political place. A searing memory: returning home from my elementary school to find my stepfather nodding off, with a needle in his arm. A memory that I would relive in my own body—as a young adult I too became a "user." Raised in violence, I enacted my own upon the world and upon myself. What saved me was the camera—its ability to gaze upon, to focus, to investigate, to reclaim, to resist, to re-envision. I see my photographs as reflections of these experiences: generations of violence, adolescents in prison, and families of the incarcerated.

In 1992 I began photographing gangs in Los Angeles, leading to my book "East Side Stories: Gang Life in East L.A.," published in 1998. At that time, it was one of the first photography books to take a long-term, deep look inside gang life in Los Angeles. This subject matter was very attractive to mainstream media. I was adamant that this book be more than just photographs. I fought hard to include texts that explained the history of Los Angeles and its complexities of gang culture. I wanted to give context to the lives depicted in this book and take a leading role in guiding young readers from such communities to re-envision their futures. I made sure that students were included in tours of my Los Angeles Gangs exhibition at the International Center of Photography. I became a spokesman for this subject matter in interviews with CNN, PBS, NPR, BBC, and Univision. I then realized the impact of this project and began to lecture about these topics at schools and universities around the country.

-Joseph Rodriguez

http://josephrodriguezphotography.com

Joseph Rodriguez was born and raised in Brooklyn, New York. He began studying photography at the School of Visual Arts and went on to receive an Associate of Applied Science at New York City Technical College. He worked in the graphic arts industry before deciding to pursue photography further. In 1985 he graduated with a Photojournalism and Documentary Diploma from the International Center of Photography in New York. He went on to work for Black Star photo agency, and print and online news organizations like National Geographic, The New York Times Magazine, Mother Jones, Newsweek, Esquire, Stern, and New America Media. He has received awards and grants from the New York Foundation for the Arts, Artists' Fellowship, USC Annenberg Institute for Justice and Journalism, the Open Society Institute Justice Media Fellowship and Katrina Media Fellowship, National Endowment for the Arts, the Rockefeller Foundation, Mother Jones International Fund for Documentary Photography, and the Alicia Patterson Fellowship Fund for Investigative Journalism. He has been awarded Pictures of the Year by the National Press Photographers Association and the University of Missouri, in 1990, 1992, 1996 and 2002. He is the author of Spanish Harlem, part of the "American Scene" series, by the National Museum of American Art/ D.A.P., as well as East Side Stories: Gang Life in East Los Angeles, Juvenile, Flesh Life Sex in Mexico City, and Still Here: Stories After Katrina, Powerhouse Books. Recent exhibitions include the Hardhitta Gallery, Cologne, Germany; Irene Carlson Gallery of Photography, University of La Verne, California; Third Floor Gallery, Cardiff, Wales, UK Institute for Public Knowledge, New York, NY; Moving Walls, Open Society Institute, New York, NY; and Cultural Memory Matters, 601 Art Space, New York, NY.

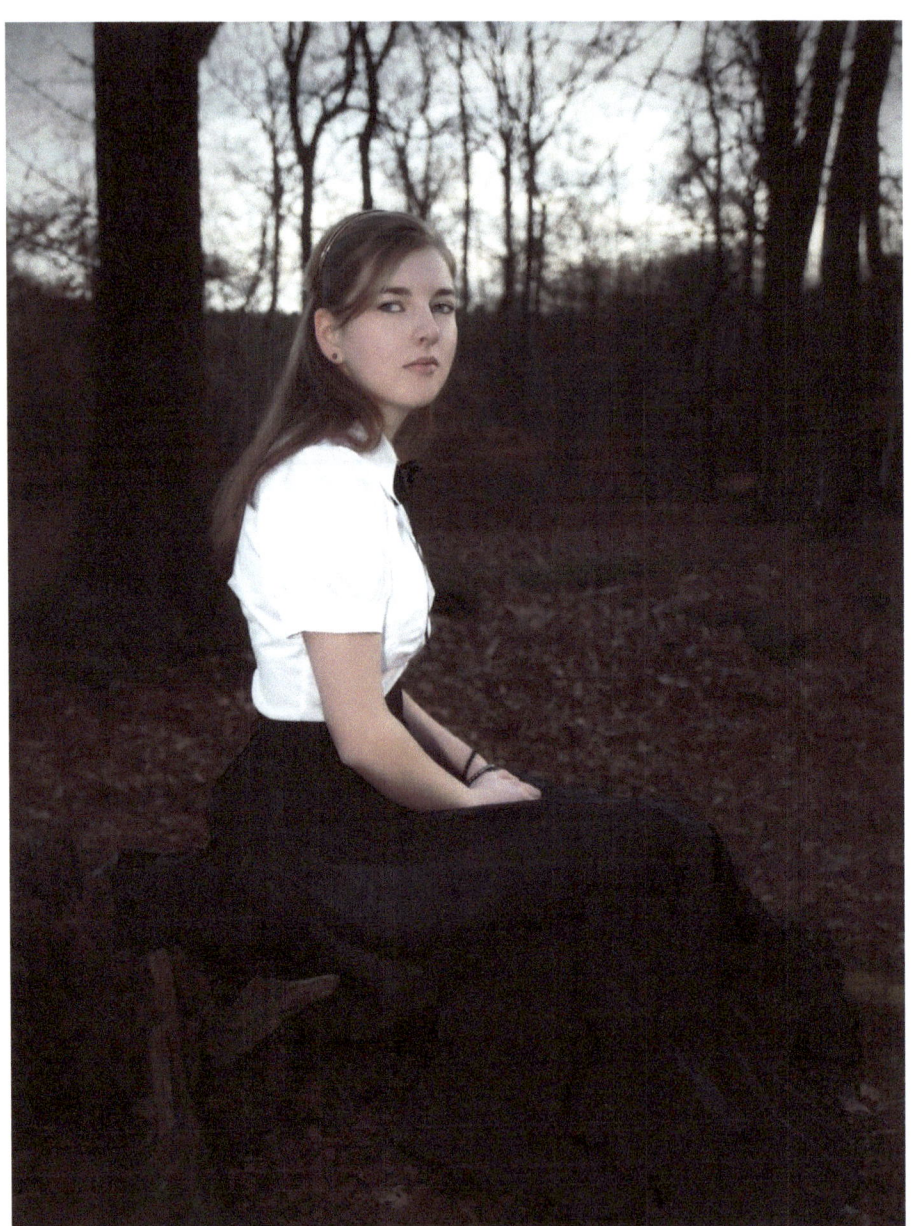

Christopher Kamper, *In Real Life*, 2008, photobook, 80 pages, 22.86 cm x 17.78 cm, perfect binding, full-colour interior ink. Copyright: Christopher Kamper c/o LSBU BA Digital Photography.

Paula Roush

Download Fever

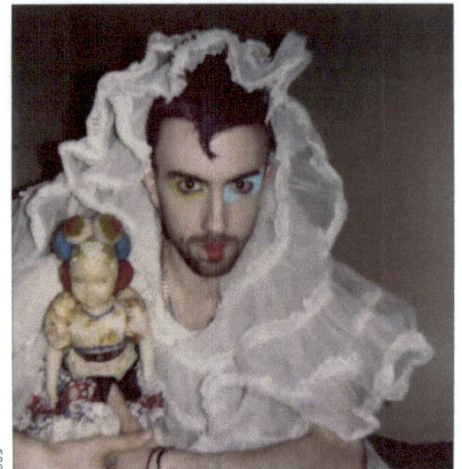
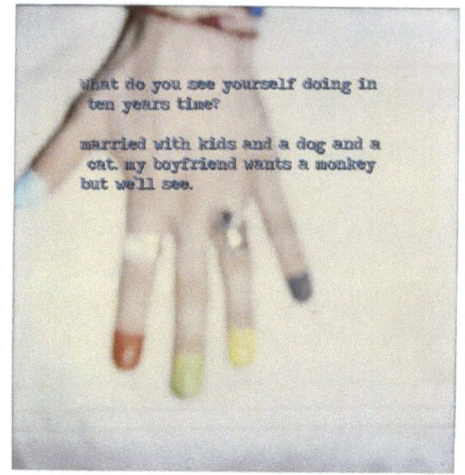

What do you see yourself doing in ten years time?

married with kids and a dog and a cat. my boyfriend wants a monkey but we'll see.

what do you work at now both creatively and otherwise?

i work at not forgetting that others cant see what is in my head.

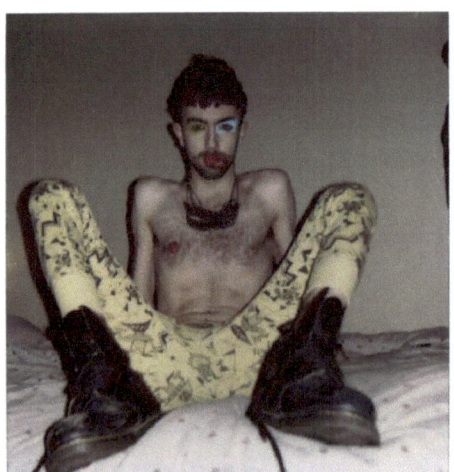

Robbie Sweeney, *Our Creative Youth*, 2008, photobook, 115 pages, 15.24 cm © 22.86 cm, casewrap-hardcover binding, full-colour interior ink. Copyright: Robbie Sweeney c/o LSBU BA Digital Photography.

Representing post-subcultures

With its point of departure in a box containing Anita Corbin's travelling exhibition "Visible Girls" (1981), the selected photobooks are part of a self-publishing project with young people (2007-2009), with the aim of creating a counter-archive of current youth culture. The photobooks reveal our engagement with archival practices and the research of personal everyday histories that cross online–offline spaces. These work as counter-memory narratives (Foucault); narratives that are counter to academic, media and state accounts of youth culture as shaped by institutional agendas and moral panics.

The "Visible Girls" is best understood in relation to sociological studies of youth in the 1980s. It was, at that time, a reaction to the context of seminal subcultural studies then taking place and their focus on male subcultural style (see, for example, Subculture: The Meaning of Style by Dick Hebdige). Anita Corbin argues in "Visible Girls" that girls had been largely underrepresented in subcultural studies, echoing the 1980s feminist critique of subcultural studies by Angela McRobbie. Now, applying a feminist perspective to the reinterpretation of the box Girls Subcultures meant a number of things: a continued investigation of patriarchal meanings in representations of youth cultures; a questioning of rigid dualities in gender definitions; the implications of ambiguous sexuality; and a continuing questioning of gender identities and "moral panic" about youth.

Additionally, earlier subcultural theory with its reliance on the relationship between social class, style and spectacular fashion has been reworked into what is now normally acknowledged as a post-subcultural studies framework. David Muggleton and Rupert Weinzierl suggest that the days "of working class youth sub-cultures 'heroically' resisting subordination through 'semiotic guerrilla warfare'" are long gone. Instead, the more fluid concepts of "tribes" (Maffesoli) or "neo-tribes" (Bennett) have been capturing the experience of fragmentation, flux and fluidity that is central to contemporary youth cultures and the way "global mainstreams and local sub-streams produce new, hybrid cultural constellations."

With Corbin's "Visible Girls" at the centre of the project, the question we addressed was how to create possibilities for a post-subcultural photography. This raised two central questions: "who participates in contemporary youth post-subcultures?" and "are girls still invisible and if so how can we articulate this in/visibility in the light of the impact of global networked technologies?"

-Paula Roush

Extracts from: Paula Roush, 2009. *Download fever: photography, subcultures and online-offline counter-archival strategies*, In A. Dewdney and M. Lister eds, Photographies, 2 (2), London:Taylor & Francis, pp 143-167.

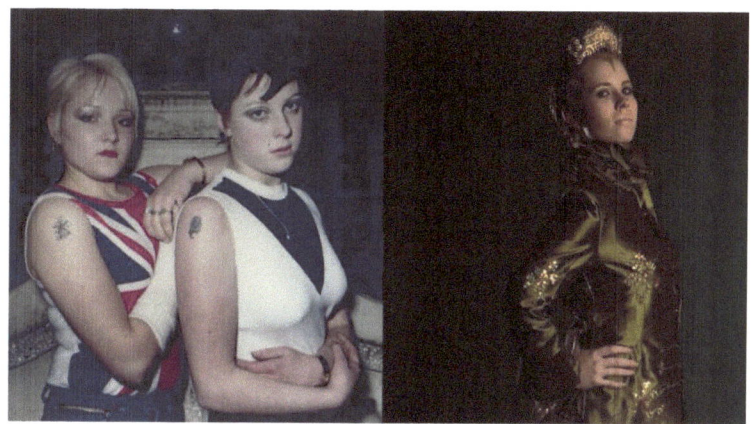

Anita Corbin, *Visible Girls*, 1981. One of 26 photographs in the exhibition panels, with introduction and audiotape Conversation with the Girls, part of the box GS Girls Subcultures, Cockpit Gallery/ Camerawork archives. Copyright: Anita Corbin c/o LSBU BA Digital Photography.R: Lee Slaymaker , The Pop Cosmopolitanist: A Blank Canvas, 2009, photobook, 54 pages, 15.24 cm x 22.86 cm, saddle-stitch binding, full-colour interior ink. Copyright: Lee Slaymaker c/o LSBU BA Digital Photography.

Paula Roush was born in Lisbon and is currently based in London where she works as an artist and educator. Her work explores the aesthetics of installation art, referencing history, collective memory and forgetfulness, the materiality of archives and gendered subjectivities. Additionally the focus of her academic research is the photobook, artists' publications and self-publishing. Two of her ongoing projects are: THE FOUND PHOTO FOUNDATION, shown at Dear Aby Warburg, What can be done with images? Museum für Gegenwartskunst Siegen, 2012- 2013; and THE PAST PERSISTS IN THE PRESENT IN THE FORM OF A DREAM (PARTICIPATORY ARCHITECTURES, ARCHIVE AND REVOLUTION), shown at the Guatephoto, Guatemala City, 2012, The Brighton Photo Fringe and The Brighton Photo Biennial 12 Photobook Show, 2012. She is a Fulbright alumni and a lecturer at the London South Bank University and the University of Westminster.

www.msdm.org.uk

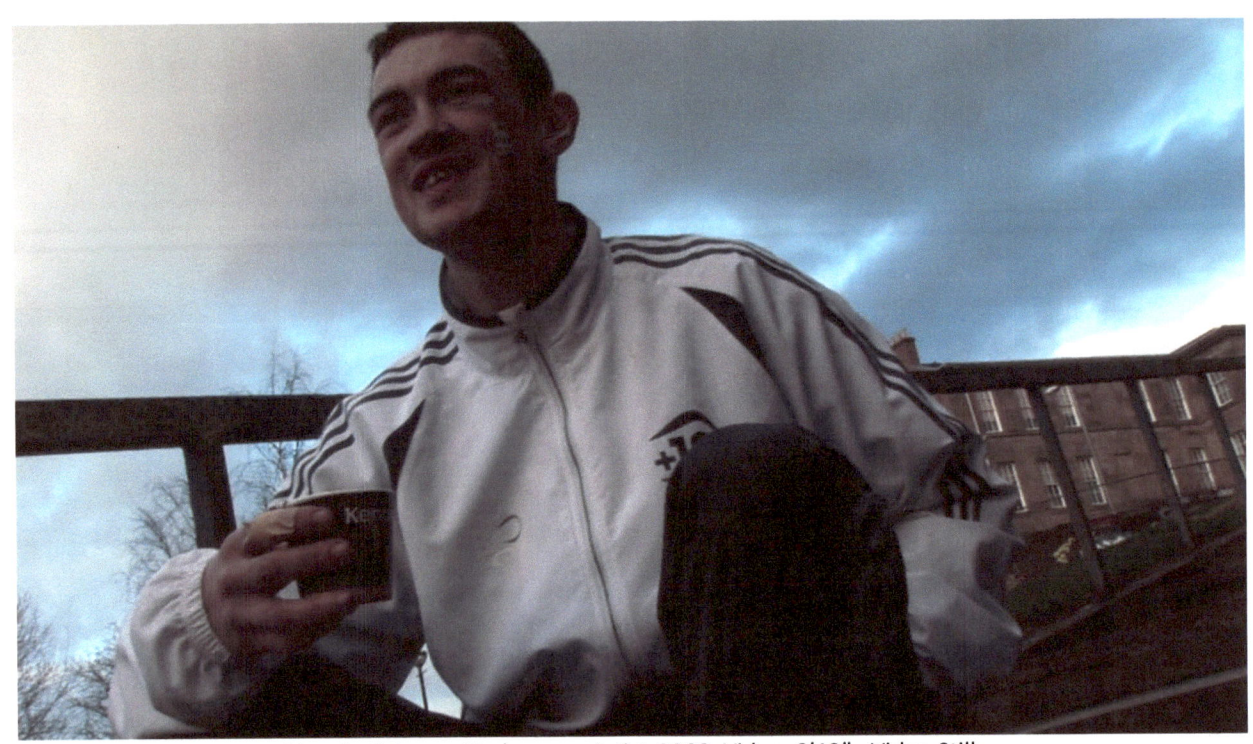

Maayke Schurer, *Undercover Artist,* 2008. Video, 3'13". Video Still.

Maayke Schurer

Undercover Artist

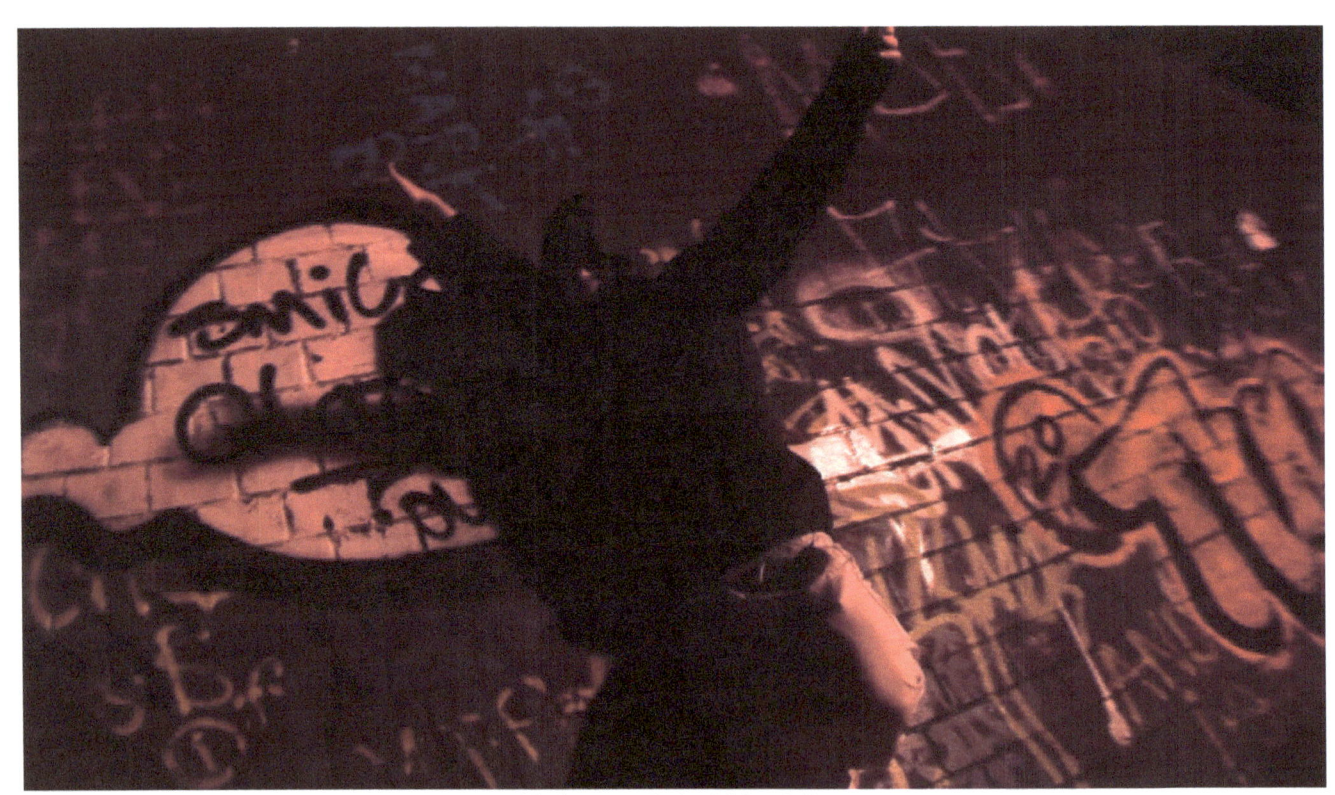

Undercover Artist, Video Still.

Undercover Artist

An impromptu music video made while walking home alone one night in Glasgow. What starts as harassment from members of a young team (aka NED's) evolves into an on the spot collaborative shoot. This is the first of a series that follows these youths over the next few weeks until Bernard (the singer in this video) is stabbed and killed.

Maayke Schurer is a Dutch Canadian artist who graduated from the Glasgow School of Art and is currently working and living in Ottawa, Canada. **www.maayke.com**

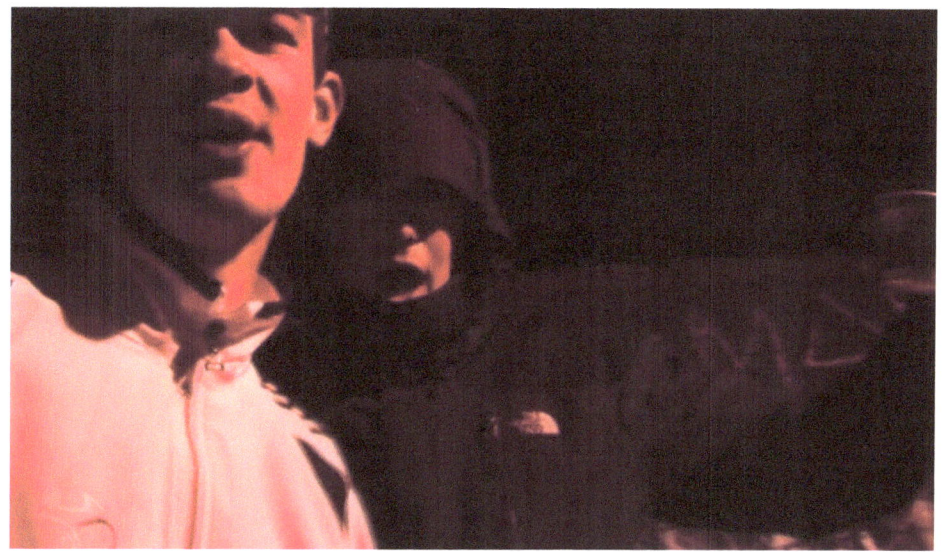

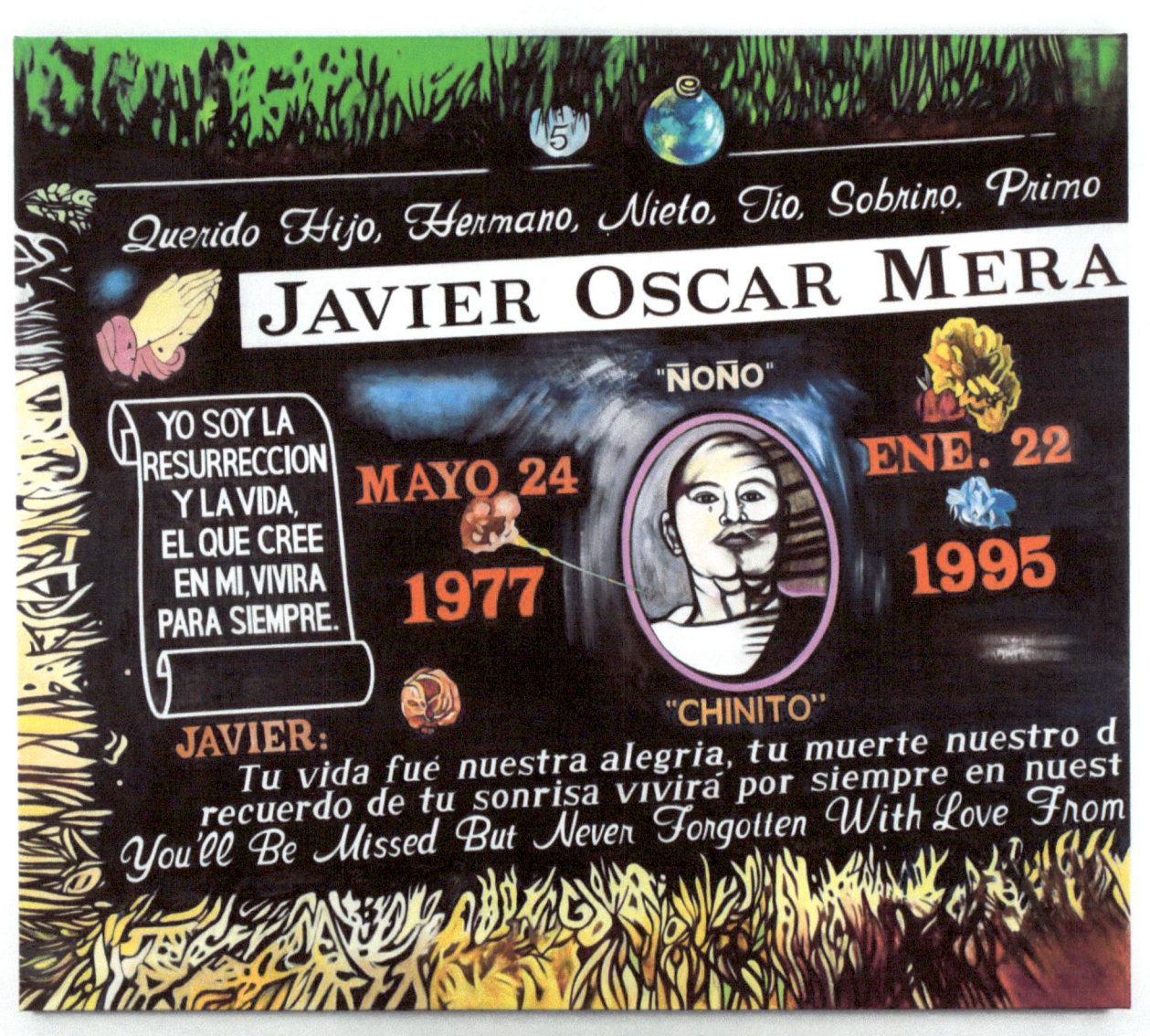

Robert Taub, *Our Beloved Homeboy*, 2005-2006. Oil on linen, 83 x 99 inches.

Robert Taub

Resurrection Cemetery

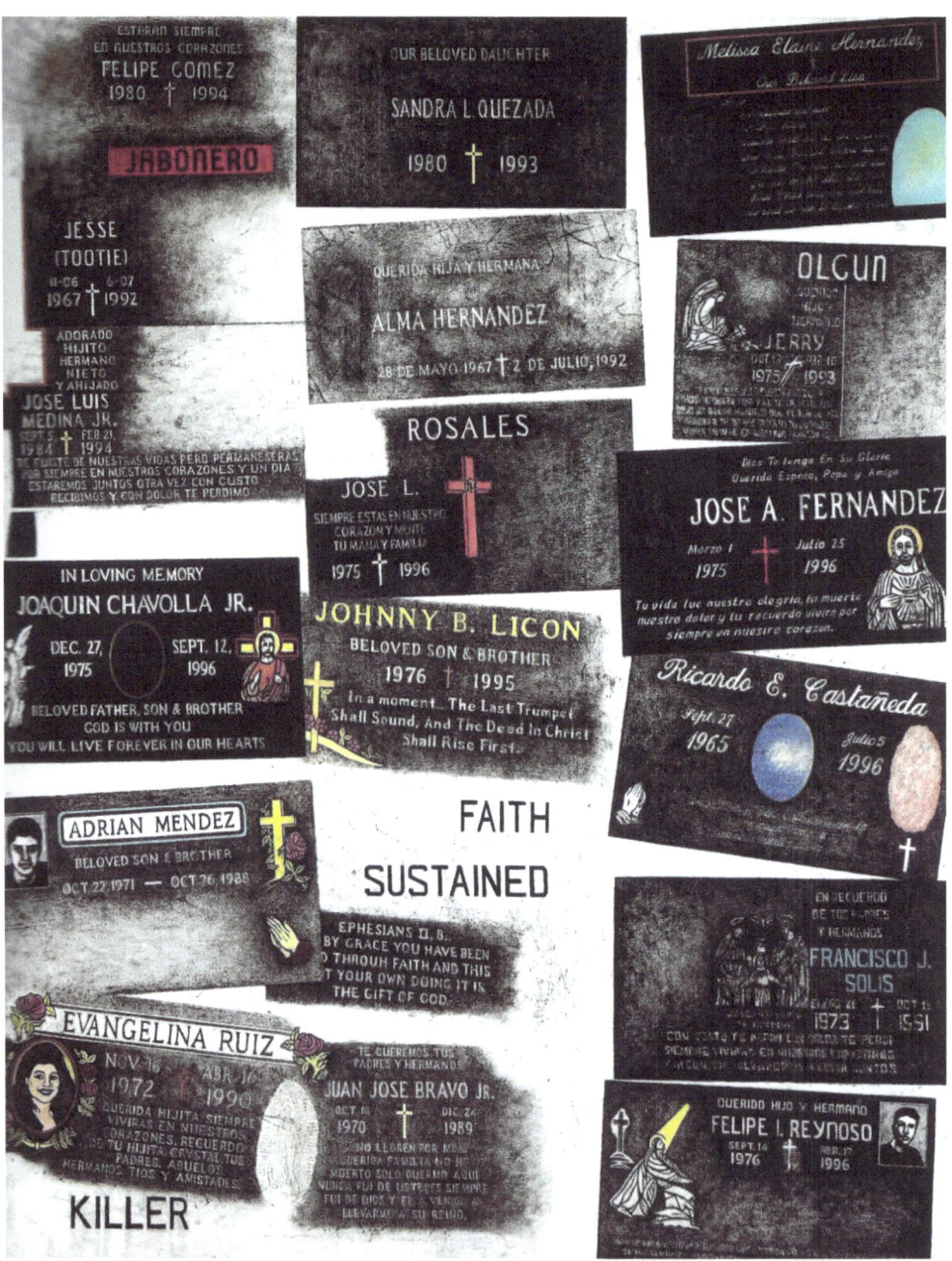

Robert Taub, *ECCE HOMO*, 2000. Crayon and oil on canvas, 100 x 80 inches.

Resurrection Cemetery

The genesis of *Resurrection Cemetery* (2007) goes back to when I was living in LA and working as a substitute teacher. I noticed a fair number of students in wheelchairs and sweaters with Old English lettering that began with "In Loving Memory." A student in my class was killed. I started talking with some of the students about it and soon realized they were part of a war going on in the streets of LA.

Around this time I heard Father Gregory Boyle, founder of Homeboy Industries, interviewed on the radio. He talked about his work with gangs and about the 87 and counting people he had personally buried. I decided to do a memorial project of headstone rubbings on canvas documenting the people Father Boyle had buried.

I contacted Father Boyle and he gave me his connections, assistance and blessing. I called this project "Life and Death in East LA."

The vast majority of gang related homicides are buried in the "R" section of Resurrection Cemetery. While I was working there at Christmas the area became enveloped in a mass of color, motion, texture and symbolism...pinwheels, balloons, confetti, baby animals, baby Jesuses, dice, artifacts, messages, rosaries, little Virgin Marys, toys. An outpouring of remembrance, grief and celebration.

Over time I took a large number of photos. In the studio I blew up the photographs and created a new series of paintings based on these photos, *Resurrection Cemetery*, 2007.

-Robert Taub

Robert Taub grew up in South Philadelphia. He attended UC Berkeley and the University of Pennsylvania, where he studied fine arts and philosophy and earned an MFA degree.

Taub has lived in and travelled extensively in Mexico, Africa, Japan, the Middle East, Europe and the United States. He currently resides in Brooklyn, NY.

His work has been exhibited widely, including recent exhibitions in New York, Los Angeles, Mexico and East Africa.

www.roberttaub.com

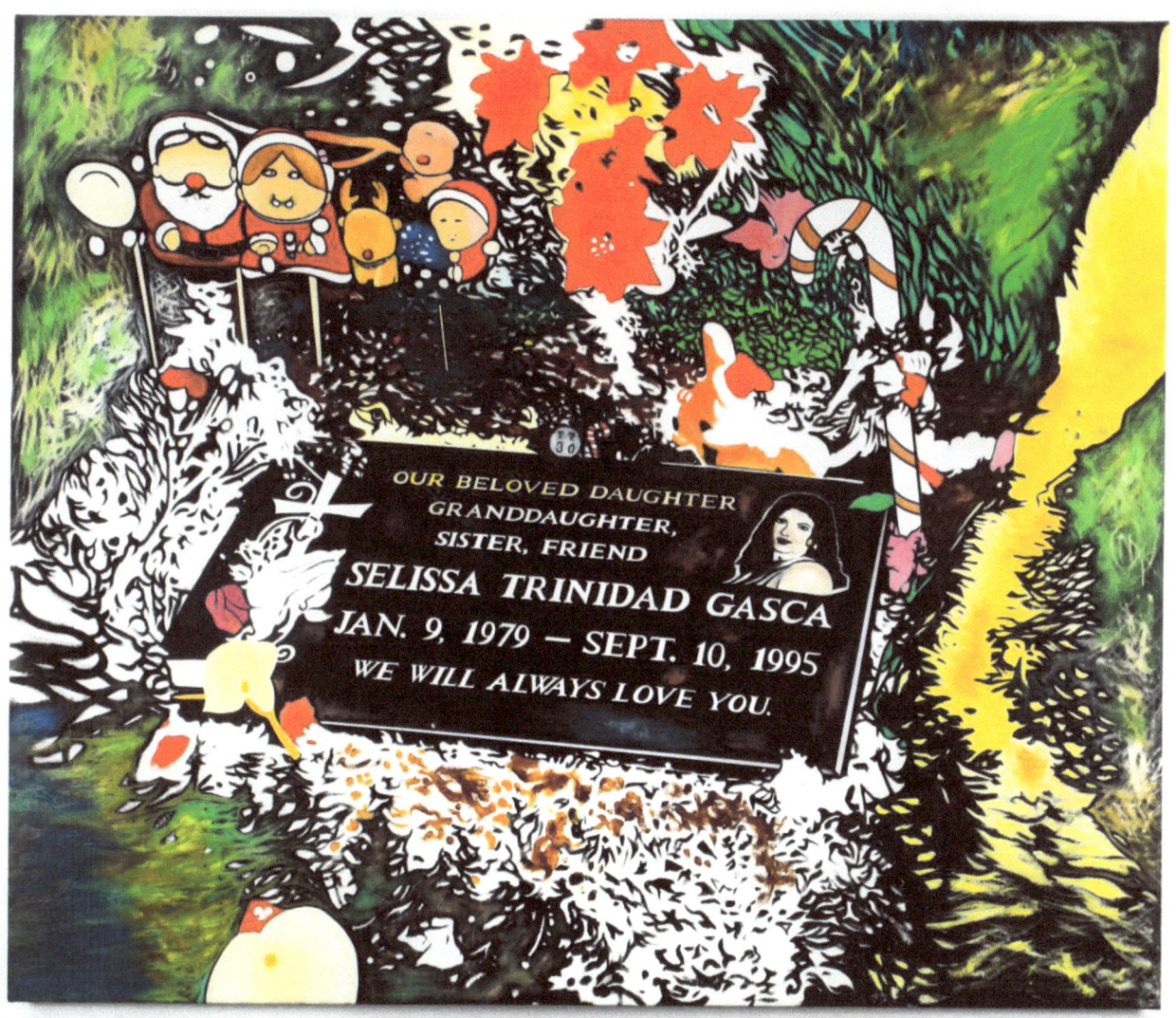

Robert Taub, *Of Ice Cream and Birthday Parties*, 2005-2006. Oil on linen, 83 x 98 inches.

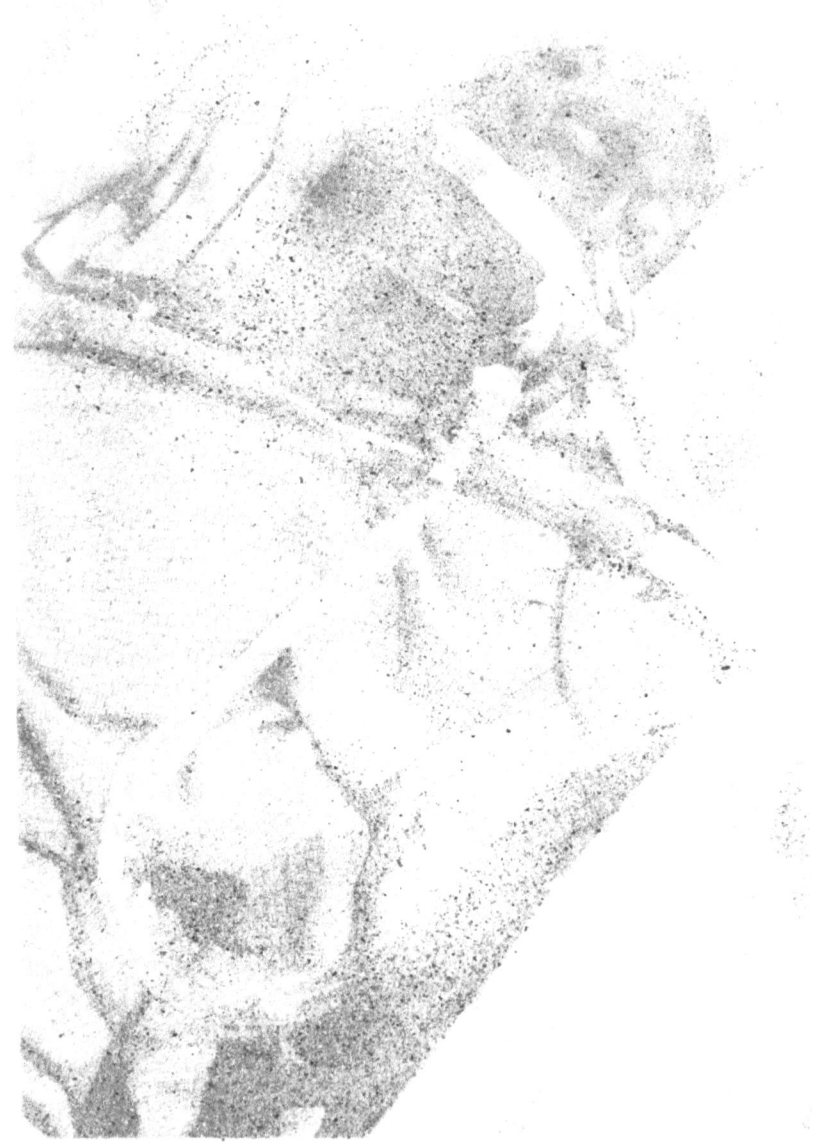

Zefrey Throwell, *Douglas Throwell #16, 59 Years Old*, 2013. Human Ash, methamphetamine, acrylic   on canvas, 48 x 36 inches. Image courtesy of Klemens Gasser & Tanja Grunert, Inc.

Zefrey Throwell

At last...rest

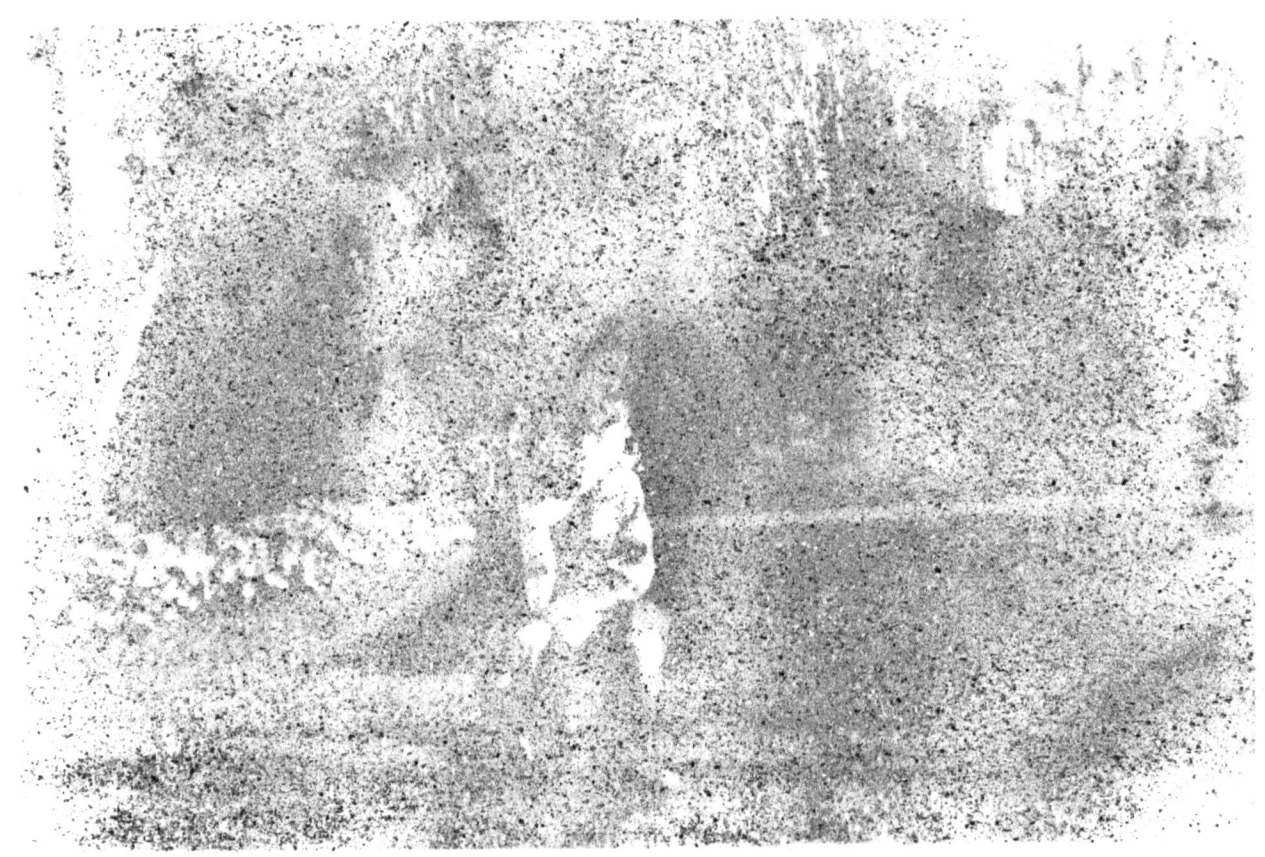

Douglas Throwell #9, 7 Years Old, 2013. Human ash, methamphetamine, acrylic on canvas, 38 x 36 inches. Image courtesy of Klemens Gasser & Tanja Grunert, Inc.

At last…rest

At last…rest is a series of eight large-scale portraits, memorials to Throwell's father, painted using his cremated ashes that contain traces of the methamphetamine that ended his life. The technique of painting moments of his father's life with his ashes in *At last…rest*, utilizes its own material qualities, capturing the soft focus of memory, locked in expectation and sublime contemplation. They span his father's life: his rough upbringing and running away from home at age 15, life as a hippy in Haight-Ashbury in the 60's, smuggling drugs as a biker in the 80's, and finally his death of a meth overdose at age 59. Throwell's paintings lovingly embrace and reflect on the inevitable catastrophe.

The most dangerous drug in the world - crystal, crank, Tina, methamphetamine or more commonly known as meth. The epidemic of meth use that has infected the United States is now spreading to Europe and the rest of the world. Destroying the lives of individuals, families and communities, meth threatens to undo the very fabric of our world.

Zefrey Throwell's recent performances are rooted in astute social criticism, aggressively reclaiming private space for public use with a focus on convivial community spirit, aka fun. Often the performances involve massive groups of people, such as the largest and loudest symphony in history— the 1,000 car horn orchestration entitled Entropy Symphony III with LAND in Los Angeles and a weeklong strip poker critique of modern economics called I'll Raise You One... for Performa 11 at Art in General. Nine of Throwell's films, including Ocularpation: Wall Street, have been screened at the Museum of Modern Art for a special night honoring Throwell's work curated by Rajendra Roy, chief curator of film at MoMA. Throwell's first major museum presentation at the Leopold Hoesch Museum in Dueren, Germany 2012 included the film Time Stau, At last...rest. Throwell's new artist book "Folding Space/Pressing Time" is a collaboration with artist Dan Gluibizzi and can be acquired at the gallery or through the artist's web page **www.zefrey.com.** *Throwell's projects have been featured in The New York Times, CNN, NPR, NBC, Artforum, Art in America and Modern Painters. Throwell has work in The Museum of Modern Art, NY collection and other major collections around the world.*[57]   **www.zefrey.com**

---

[57] Text and Images courtesy of Klemens Gasser & Tanja Grunert, 524 W. 19TH ST NY, NY 10011, Zefrey Throwell's exhibition: Panic in the Chalk Cave. February 28 – March 23, 2013. www.grassergruner.net.

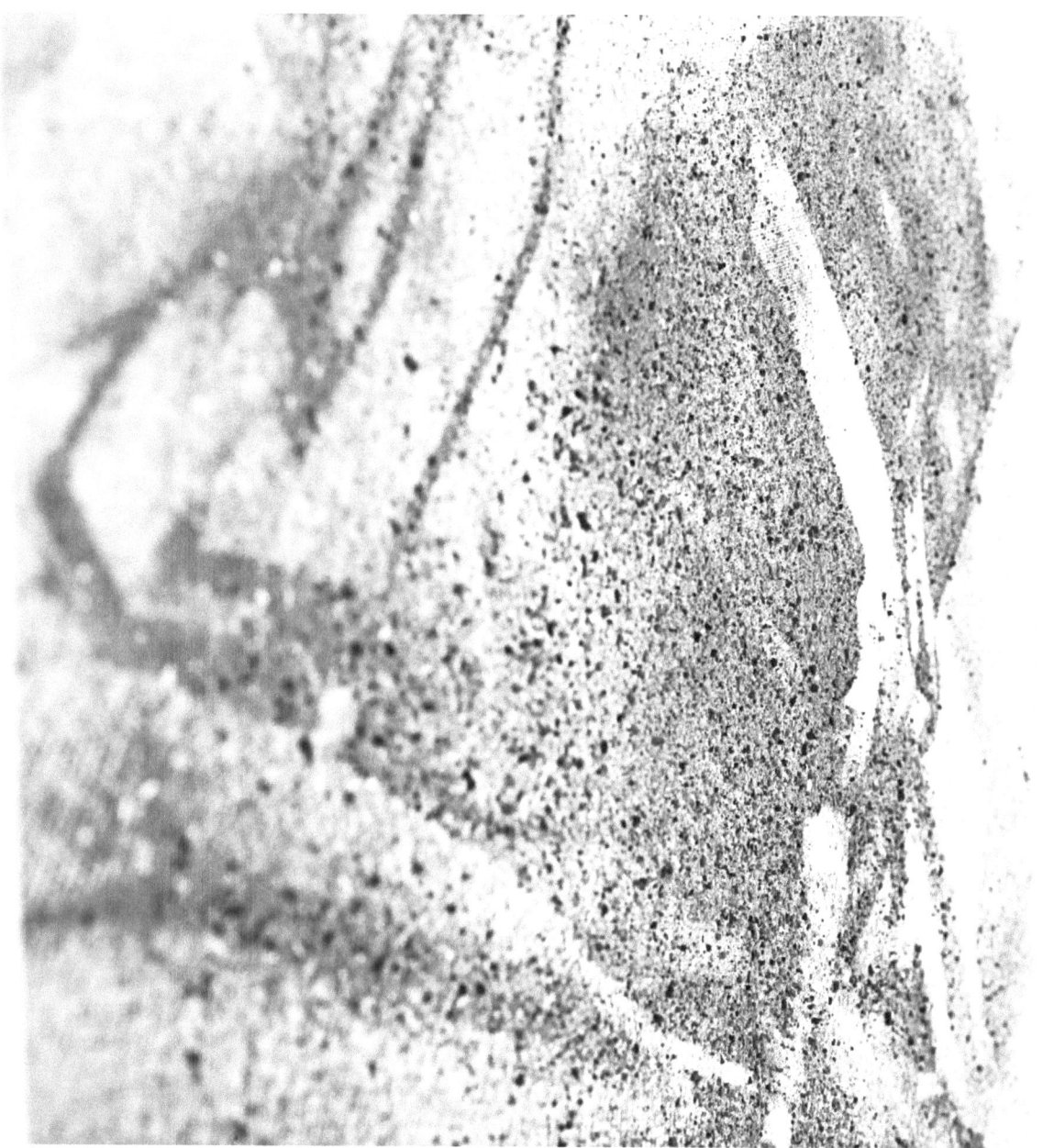

Douglas Throwell #16, 59 Years Old, 2013. Human Ash, methamphetamine, acrylic on canvas, 48 x 36 inches, detail. Image courtesy of Klemens Gasser & Tanja Grunert, Inc.

Credits

Paula Roush's archive of photographic collections includes books by the following artists: Rachel Johnson, Tim Body, Robbie Sweeny, Lee Slaymaker, MJ Gumayagay, Richard Harris, Christopher Kamper, Richard Johnson, Natalie Cheung, Karel Polt, Dana Mendonca, Charlotte Miceli, and Rich Harley.

AC Institute
547 W. 27th St. #210

Ceiling Height 10' 7"

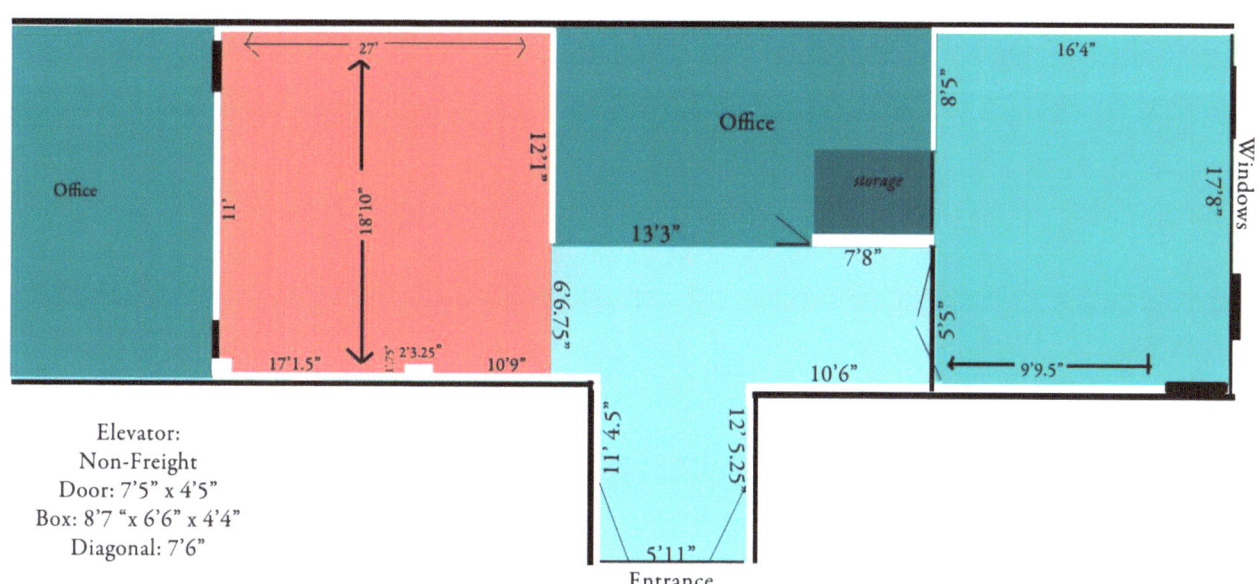

Elevator:
Non-Freight
Door: 7'5" x 4'5"
Box: 8'7 "x 6'6" x 4'4"
Diagonal: 7'6"

www.ingramcontent.com/pod-product-compliance
Lightning Source LLC
Chambersburg PA
CBHW050852180526
45159CB00007B/2656